a directory for home design

materials

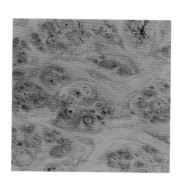

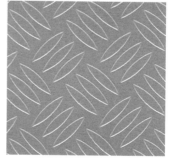

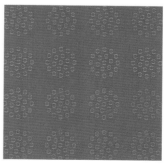

Elizabeth Wilhide

materials a directory

r home design

Quadrille

Editorial Director: Anne Furniss
Creative Director: Mary Evans
Designer: Paul Welti
Project Editor: Hilary Mandleberg
Production: Nancy Roberts
Picture Research: Nadine Bazar
Picture Assistant: Sarah Airey

First published in 2001 by
Quadrille Publishing Limited
Alhambra House
27–31 Charing Cross Road
London WC2H 0LS

British Library Cataloguing-in-Publication
Data
A catalogue record for this book is
available from the British Library.

ISBN 1 9038451 14

Printed and bound in China

contents

introduction

Contemporary design places the focus on material quality. While traditional styles of decorating have tended to emphasize applied finishes, today's interiors allow the unique characteristics of wood, stone, glass and metal to speak for themselves. From smooth matt plywood to translucent perspex, from cool, classic limestone to burnished concrete, the scope has never been greater. Materials once considered suitable only for industrial or commercial use have found a new, expressive role in the modern home.

Designing with materials creates effects which are more than skin deep. Unlike superficial transformations with paper or paint, the robust use of materials as cladding, surfaces or integral elements offers a basic integrity that outlasts trends in interior fashion. Evocative combinations of glass and metal, wood and stone create sympathetic backgrounds with inbuilt liveliness and variety and the potential to improve with wear and time. From floors and walls, to screens, worksurfaces, doors and details, the sheer range of applications provides a host of opportunities to add an enduring sense of character to the interior.

The material aesthetic

Material quality has always been embedded in the process of design. When a designer, a builder, an architect or a craftsperson chooses a material, to a great extent they are also choosing how a design will look, how it will perform and how it will last. At the same time, the physical properties of materials inherently shape what you can do with them, perameters particularly familiar to anyone involved in the process of hand-making. Designing with materials is thus not merely a question of making an appropriate selection but is more in the nature of a two-way exchange.

If the physical characteristics of materials have a bearing on design, their associative qualities also provoke a response. Materials have inbuilt values that arise from context and application, meanings that resonate and add depth to a scheme. In many cases, these qualities are the result of centuries of familiarity.

A basic distinction is commonly drawn between materials that are rare, expensive and hence 'luxurious', and those which are more commonplace and readily available. Centuries before mass production and worldwide transport links, it was those materials that could be obtained locally – timber from forested areas or stone from nearby quarries – which were chiefly used in construction, an expediency that gave rise to the rich variety of vernacular traditions around the world. The sun-baked adobe houses of Mexico, the timber-framed clapboard houses of New England, the brick and flint cottages of the Thames Valley and the stone farmhouses of northwest France have one thing in common: they all make use of local materials. But what was for our ancestors simply a question of practicality and economic good sense can be seen today as delivering a more significant benefit. Houses fashioned from local materials seem almost to grow out of the landscape: they have a 'rightness' and a rootedness that is not easily achieved in other ways.

From earliest times, the use of materials has also provided a means of signifying power and status. At the most obvious, princes and prelates could advertise their wealth and authority by employing rare, imported materials in the construction or decoration of their palaces. Equally, the same richness could be expressed decoratively, by working 'humble' materials in elaborate ways. An ornate and intricate rood screen, for example, might have been made from

the same type of wood as the rough-hewn beams in a country farmhouse, but the material in each case is sending out very different messages. This implied hierarchy of material quality – which would place imported Italian marble, for instance, above locally quarried sandstone in terms of value and significance – has been responsible for a significant strand in the history of interior decoration. By the eighteenth century, with the rise of the gentry, those who could not afford the finest and most expensive materials but wished to convey the same sense of richness often turned to some form of artifice: wooden firesurrounds, for example, might be 'marbled' in paint, or softwood grained and stained to suggest hardwood. Almost every rare and exotic material imaginable, from tortoiseshell to porphyry, has found its counterpart in a decorative paint technique.

The industrial revolution in the early nineteenth century and the development of new manufacturing methods and materials brought a whole new dimension to decorative simulation. A burgeoning middle class was able to decorate and furnish their homes in imitation of the rich, even if the effect was only skin-deep. Dickens' *nouveau riche* couple in *Our Mutual Friend*, pointedly called the Veneerings, embody the showy, inauthentic taste of the upwardly mobile Victorian. And, as the century wore on and Britain's imperial power reached its zenith, exotic materials from colonial outposts were added to the mix, materials such as bamboo and rattan.

Reaction was not long in coming. William Morris and his followers in the Arts and Crafts Movement, who built on the earlier ideas of John Ruskin, attacked 'sham' styles of decoration and the mass-produced mediocrity of consumer goods pumped out of nineteenth-century factories with what amounted to a moral fervour. As a young man, William Morris had been conspicuously unimpressed by the Great Exhibition of 1851, the triumphal showcase for Britain's new industries. 'Shoddy is King,' he observed, and refused even to enter the Crystal Palace where the Exhibition was held. Little more than a decade later, when Morris first set up in business with a number of like-minded friends, he advocated a return to pre-industrial ways of working, a revival of the traditional crafts that industrialization had brought to the brink of extinction. In the design and decoration of Red House, Morris's first home, many of these radical ideas were first expressed.

The ideas of Morris and his followers represent a significant shift in the material aesthetic. Red House was both richly decorated with handmade embroidered wall hangings, stencilling and painted furniture, and at the same time shockingly unadorned. From the choice of a warm local brick as the principal material of construction – a choice which gave the house its name – to the exposed oak beams, brick arches and plain whitewashed walls of the interior, Red House made a strong statement about the integrity of materials. 'Grand and severely simple', in the estimation of one visitor, the house enshrined the notion of 'honesty' in design and decoration, a value judgement which has rarely been absent from any discussion about material quality ever since. Marbling, veneer, imitation wood, derivative detailing were wrong; simple, country materials left in as plain a state as possible had the moral high ground. 'If any regard is to be had to the general beauty of the landscape,' wrote Morris in 1880, 'the natural material of the special landscape should be used instead of imported material.'

The Arts and Crafts movement was immensely influential, not only at home but worldwide; it could be argued that the movement has been responsible, directly or indirectly, for many of the contemporary notions about material quality we hold today. The seminal work *Das Englische Haus* by the German Hermann Muthesius introduced Arts and Crafts

interiors and architecture to a European audience. Radical European design movements of the early nineteenth century, such as the Wiener Werkstatte, founded by Josef Hoffman and Koloman Moser, embodied many Arts and Crafts ideals and practitioners cited Morris as one of their principal inspirations. Similarly, in the United States, far-sighted retailers such as Gustav Stickley were directly influenced by the work of Morris and other Arts and Crafts designers such as Lethaby and Voysey. Stickley's 'Mission' style of furniture, robust designs in oak that celebrated the pioneer life, were enormously successful in establishing an emergent American material sensibility.

By the end of the century, the honest use of humble materials had lost its capacity to shock and had become something positively to admire. Sir Edwin Lutyens' early houses in the Arts and Crafts or vernacular idiom elevated the use of local or humble materials to an art form. Surrey houses such as Munstead Wood or Orchards (described as a 'symphony of local materials') were typically constructed of local 'rubble' stone, a type of sandstone, set off with red tile and oak. The massive oak beams that support Munstead Wood, the house Lutyens designed for the great garden designer Gertrude Jekyll, were hewn from trees that once grew only a mile and a half away: 'There is the actual living interest of knowing where the trees one's house is built of really grew,' she wrote. While Lutyens' use of local materials had its roots in the Arts and Crafts notion of 'honesty', he well understood the ability of such materials to convey a sense of settled permanence. Lutyens' new houses never looked new; they had an aura of belonging, which is precisely what his clients wanted.

Another architect to make expressive use of humble materials was Frank Lloyd Wright. But whereas Lutyens used materials to suggest a history, Wright's purposes were more elemental: to wed the house to the land. His early Prairie Houses with their timber frames and long, low horizontal lines had a pioneering spirit; his use of rugged materials, such as freestone or fieldstone, suggests the power of nature in the raw. Fallingwater, Wright's most famous and perhaps his finest house, is the ultimate expression of organic architecture. Built over a waterfall, the core of the house is a massive freestone chimney and hearth built onto solid rock. In later works, he used pierced and perforated concrete components in a similarly organic, expressive way, dissolving the boundary between interior and exterior spaces.

The materials that have defined twentieth-century design, however, are not the familiar, 'honest' Arts and Crafts elements of timber and local stone but brash, new manufactured materials such as reinforced concrete, steel and plate

left Designed by John Pawson, this minimal kitchen features a single worksurface made of Italian limestone which extends right through into the adjacent garden. The flooring is also Italian limestone.

glass. The result of huge advances in technology and manufacturing methods, these machine age materials have made possible entirely new forms of building. The plasticity of concrete gives us the fluid spiral of Wright's Guggenheim Museum in New York or the soaring wings of Saarinen's TWA terminal at John F. Kennedy International Airport, New York; the transparent Farnsworth House in Illinois by Mies van der Rohe, with its minimal structural steel frame, has walls that are mere infills of glass.

Just as humble materials acquired moral value for Arts and Crafts practitioners, the new materials of the twentieth century became emblematic of progress. Le Corbusier, in his modernist manifesto, *Towards a New Architecture*, argued passionately in favour of replacing natural materials with artificial ones. For Le Corbusier, artificial materials were the materials of economy and reason; they could be fabricated on site or in factories to meet exact specifications and opened up the possibility of mass-produced housing. With artificial materials, the house could be conceived as a 'tool', a 'machine for living'. And not just houses: contemporary designers since Le Corbusier – such as Charles and Ray Eames, Harry Bertoia, Achille Castiglioni and Eero Saarinen have conceived furniture, lights and other interior fittings in tubular steel, punched aluminium, moulded plywood, polypropylene and a host of other twentieth-century material innovations.

In recent decades, the modernist material aesthetic has lead inevitably to a whole new dichotomy. In place of 'rich' and 'poor' materials, or honest (bare) and decorated (covered up), a new dividing line has now been drawn between natural and synthetic. This opposition has been given added emphasis by postwar developments in the plastics industries and the introduction of a range of new artificial materials that offer both infinite possibilities in terms of form and considerable practical advantages in terms of maintenance and durability. But it has been the use of plastics to simulate the visual qualities of 'real' materials, together with their demonstrably adverse impact on the global environment, that has more recently caused a certain reappraisal of their true value. Natural, once again, has become a term of approbation, and the qualities that set natural materials apart from artificial ones – such as the fact that they age and weather, betraying the marks of time – are positively welcomed as marks of authenticity.

Like all the other oppositions which have defined the way we look at materials, the distinction between 'natural' and 'artificial' is far from clearcut. Many natural materials are processed industrially; some synthetics have a high

proportion of natural ingredients. Nor is it easier to make firm value judgements. To take one example, natural materials are popularly assumed to be better than artificial ones because they cause less harm to the planet. But although stone is a natural material, it must be quarried, worked and transported, processes that consume great amounts of energy; furthermore, stone is not an renewable resource. Arguably deforestation, particularly of tropical hardwoods, has been responsible for greater ecological damage than than that caused by the plastics industries. Some designers, notably Philippe Starck, argue that the use of certain types of plastic is more environmentally friendly in the long run than the use of their natural counterparts. Then, again, the decline of heavy industries and the departure of manufacturing from urban centres has inspired a certain degree of sympathy for rugged industrial or commercial materials whatever their origin: the superficial brutality of the contemporary loft, with its exposed brickwork, raw concrete and steel joists, is much softened by nostalgia. It was in such surroundings that the short-lived style high-tech arose, with its uncompromising and ironic use of hard-edged functional materials such as studded rubber flooring, toughened glass and glass brick, metal treadplate and brightly coloured plastic. While high-tech as an interior fashion did not last very long, its enduring impact has been the further blurring of boundaries between industrial/commercial and domestic spheres. In this context, highly processed materials such as steel and aluminium almost acquire the status of 'natural' simply because their use is so familiar.

What is clear, despite such apparent contradictions, is that our relationship with materials is long and complex, and that it is a relationship informed by layers of meaning: notions of progress and improvement, honesty and authenticity, richness and status. In the future, no doubt, new materials will bring other values to the fore, just as they will inspire new forms, while those materials that have existed for millennia will continue to evoke a sense of continuity and reassurance. In one sense, design always goes hand in hand with material quality. Designing without materials is almost inconceivable.

Surface and finish

The recent popularity of television makeover programmes, where enthusiastic participants transform rooms in a matter of hours, has only served to promote the idea of interior decoration as a form of consumption, as immediately gratifying as shopping. At the same time, there is the persistant notion that real design is a difficult business, best left to those who are skilled in abstract thought. Designing with materials offers an alternative route, both as a way of appreciating colours, patterns and textures in a less ephemeral fashion than slapping on a coat of paint, and as a means of grounding plans in reality, of articulating space in practical, concrete terms.

Materials engage all the senses. You can paint your walls a different colour, but you will not alter the way they feel, sound or smell. Change a floor covering, however, and a whole range of ambient factors comes into play. In many cases, material quality also adds the dimension of time. Although it can be difficult to tease out the precise cutoff point between natural and synthetic, materials such as wood and stone, terracotta and brick generally improve with use and age, mellowing sympathetically with time. This last advantage considerably offsets the principal drawback of designing with materials, which is that it often entails a higher degree of initial investment, and in some cases, effort, than other more superficial decorative cover-ups.

As with any other interior scheme, the best place to start is to assemble a palette of materials that appeal to you.

Catalogue photography, which is carefully styled and lit, can be misleading, so it is important to take the time to visit showrooms and if possible take real samples home with you for later consideration. Many outlets will provide samples in large enough sizes for you to gain some idea how a particular material will work in situ. Make sure you view these under different light conditions – by day and under artificial lighting – so that you can appreciate any tonal variations. Bear in mind that it is much more expensive and disruptive to change your mind about a particular material once it is installed than it is to have second thoughts about a paint colour. Take your time over the decision-making process.

A key factor in selection is basic practicality. Some materials suit certain locations in the home better than others. Think about qualities such as heat and sound insulation, resilience (particularly when choosing a flooring material), propensity to wear, mark or stain. Many materials require specialist help to install; with others, you may need to apply special finishes after installation or at regular intervals. Pay particular attention to the relevant section under each material that details maintenance and aftercare.

As far as aesthetics are concerned, designing with materials provides a welcome opportunity to accentuate the effects of natural light. Transparent or translucent glass, Perspex or glass brick have the obvious effect of spilling light through from area to area; shiny, reflective surfaces such as metal or glazed tile add a sparkling sense of vitality to the interior. Matt surfaces, such as pale polished stone, create serene, contemplative backdrops. But people often make the mistake of assuming that texture is more or less the only variant in a materials-based scheme. Even a superficial aquaintance with the range of materials available should be enough to demonstrate that quite strong contrasts of colour and pattern also come into play, even within the 'natural' category. With materials, colour, texture and pattern are to a large extent indivisible, a factor which gives an extra dimension to the interior. The character of a particular wood, for example, is expressed equally by its colour, its pattern of knots or grain and its surface quality, which all work together to create a sense of 'woodiness'.

Schemes which are predominantly composed of one type of material saturate you in that particular aesthetic: a kitchen that is entirely clad in stainless steel, from countertop to splashback, has all the sleek efficiency of a food laboratory; a room floored and panelled throughout in wood has all the snugness of a ship's cabin. For aficionados of a particular material, such full-on expression can be irresistible; but at the same time, the effect can also be rather overwhelming. On the practical side, if you restrict your choice largely to a single type of material, practical as well as aesthetic issues are heightened. Stone or metal clad interiors will be relentlessly hard, noisy and cold.

Richer, more livable schemes can be achieved by setting up contrasts of material character. And the beauty of this approach is that almost all materials work well together, natural or manufactured, traditional or cutting edge. The domestic, cosy familiarity of wood, for example, can be enhanced by brick or terracotta tiling or given a sharper, more contemporary edge by the introduction of metal or glass. Combinations also allow you to address different practical requirements, a factor particularly critical in the case of flooring. Where materials are combined, however, you must pay particular attention to edges and trim. Neat detailing where one material meets another is both visually and practically advantageous.

In conventional interiors, where plain plastered walls and carpeted floors have long been the norm, material variety has generally been restricted to marginal areas where an additional degree of practicality is required: the skimpy tiled splashback, for example, or wooden countertop. But materials really come into their own when they are used wholeheartedly, in sufficient quantities to make a proper, almost architectural impact. Designing with materials invites you to view the interior in terms of horizontal or vertical planes, rather than as a series of self-contained rooms. As screens, panels, levels or built-in surfaces and finishes, planes of materials articulate space in an entirely new way.

wood

left **Wood is a material which is innately comfortable and reassuring. Tongue-and-groove panelling, wide floorboards and a central storage unit clad in veneered panels make a sympathetic combination in this dressing area.**

right **A staircase made of solid ash is suspended with yacht rigging. The Moroccan couscous bowl is made of walnut; the sculptural wooden panels are antique threshing boards from Israel.**

The great Finnish architect and designer, Alvar Aalto, once described wood as 'the form-inspiring, deeply human material'. Wood may be commonplace, but it arouses an instinctive and heartfelt response. It is a material that evokes a profound sense of comfort, echoing centuries of domestic use.

Versatile, renewable and easy to work, wood has been an integral element of construction since time immemorial. For our tree-worshipping ancestors, wood was literally the stuff of life: it was not only employed to create shelters and ships, but also fuelled the sustaining, warming fires necessary for existence itself. In Norse folklore, the ash was Yggdrasil, the tree of life, while the oak was sacred to the Druids. (Both of these species could be burned in a green, or unseasoned, state and gave off little smoke.) Most significantly to ancient eyes, trees were a living resource, their endless regeneration following the cycle of the seasons.

In a more prosaic sense, both the physical characteristics of wood and its widespread availability have accounted for its dominance in the structure, finishing and cladding of buildings over the centuries – as basic frameworks, floors, roofs, doors, window frames, interior trim and panelling – not to mention its use in furniture. Relatively light, wood can be shaped and jointed to create a wide range of different types of structure, from simple huts or log cabins to more elaborate post-and-beam constructions. Stone came to be the preferred material for castles or sacred monuments, but many types of stone building – notably the classical Greek temple – actually replicated the detailing of the more temporary timber structures that had preceded them.

The domestic associations of wood derive from its widespread use around the world in the construction of ordinary houses and buildings, cottages and barns, dachas and Alpine cabins. In Europe, most houses were largely made of timber until stocks of native hardwoods began to decline in the sixteenth century. China and Japan have their own ancient traditions of timber building, evident in wooden tea houses and pavilions. Today, in areas such as Scandinavia and North America where timber is still plentiful, wood remains the most common and economic building material. From the 'shingle' style popularized by H. H. Richardson in the late nineteenth century, to the Greene brothers' development of the Californian bungalow, America has a rich tradition of domestic building in timber.

In Europe, between the fourteenth and sixteenth centuries, the architectural art of working in wood arguably reached its height. The great hammerbeam roofs of medieval halls and cathedrals, richly carved rood screens and altarpieces, and intricate half-timbered merchants' houses bear witness to a high degree of craftsmanship and skill. There was evident technological cross-fertilization, too, between the master carpenter capable of roofing a cathedral vault and the shipwright who crafted the oak-built vessels that explored the high seas – many medieval timber roofs with their massive beams and trusses resemble nothing so much as a ship's hull turned upside down.

By the sixteenth century, in the more densely populated areas of Europe, stocks of native hardwoods were in serious decline. In England, for example, Elizabeth I imposed regulations to protect supplies of oak, ash and beech for

shipbuilding, but forests continued to be consumed at a great rate. Oak, in particular, was in great demand to make charcoal, the fuel of the iron foundries. Little over a century later, many of the great forests of England had disappeared completely.

This example from history of rapid deforestation illustrates one of the inherent risks associated with the use of wood, which is the fragility of the balance between supply and demand. Today, with mechanized processes, the world is collectively consuming timber at a rate ten times faster than it can be replaced. The most disastrous consequence of this escalating consumption can be seen in the threat to areas of tropical rainforest, habitats that are home to the

majority of the world's species of flora and fauna and which serve as the green lungs of the planet. Given this precarious and worsening ecological situation, it is essential to ensure that any wood used today for whatever purpose comes from sustainable sources.

'Wood' is a blanket term that encompasses a vast range of different species, both hardwoods and softwoods, each with their own unique characteristics. For centuries, hardwoods, notably oak, teak and mahogany have been amongst the most prized of all woods, due to their strength, density and resistance to decay. Softwoods, which are less durable but quicker growing, have long been widely used as basic constructional materials and as surfaces destined for subsequent treatment, for example in the form of painting, varnishing or staining.

Today, the term 'wood' also embraces many types of manufactured products, such as plywood, medium density fibreboard (MDF), chipboard and hardboard – processed materials which have tended to be used in a workhorse capacity as linings or carcases but which are now increasingly seen as final finishes. Then there is an equivalent range of formats, everything from solid planks, tiles, strips, sheets and blocks to thinly veneered boards and panels.

As an interior finish, wood has an inherent sense of character and warmth. Wood-panelled and wood-floored rooms satisfy our basic instinct for cosiness and enclosure. The material is also reassuringly human in format and scale, with both the surface pattern of grain and figure, and the regularity of repeating boards, creating a pleasing sense of tactility and rhythm.

In terms of building, wood has long been associated with the vernacular, with traditional, country styles ranging from rustic barns to clapboard houses. But in the middle of the last century, modernist Scandinavian architects and designers such as Alvar Aalto and Arne Jacobsen brought the material right up to date, using laminated ply and teak to create original contemporary designs for interiors and furniture. Aalto's ever-popular stacking stool is a prime example. This designer's use of wood, so integral to his humane Scandinavian aesthetic, was scornfully dismissed by Mies van der Rohe as the inevitable consequence of living 'deep in a forest', but the domesticating quality of wood has undoubtedly helped to popularize this softer and more livable form of modernism. Another contemporary wood style was the stripped-pine look of the 1960s and 1970s, much associated with mass-market flat-pack furniture outlets. Stripped pine, or more often, pine that had not been covered up with paint or stain, had an unpretentious appeal that went hand in hand with the new, youthful informality of open-plan living. In recent times, darker woods, such as wenge wood, have brought an exotic note to East-West fusion styles of decorating.

Wood is one of the most companionable of all materials. This is not only the result of centuries of familiarity, but is also due to its innate physical characteristics that place it midway in the spectrum of hard and soft materials. Although by no means the most durable or longest lasting material, wood is not excessively demanding in practical terms. Cheaper, warmer, quieter, more resilient and easier to work than stone, with adequate care, wood mellows to a beautiful patina that enhances almost any style of decoration or design.

above **Rough wooden beams and a table in
yellow pine and pillar in white oak lend a robust
sense of character to a modern loft apartment.
The flooring is Douglas fir; kitchen units are
made of birch.**

wood

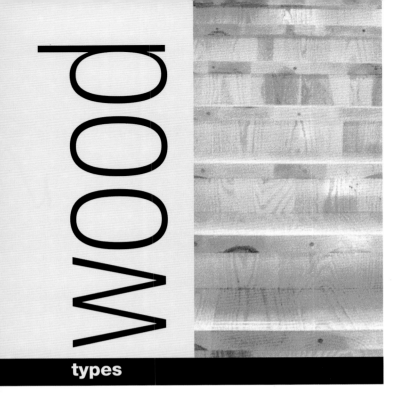

types

Wood is not a uniform material. In the days before industrialization, the ability to distinguish subtle variations from species to species, tree to tree and board to board was the stock-in-trade of master craftsmen – as a young man, the English architect Lutyens encountered a local carpenter in Surrey who could tell when an oak tree was ready for felling by the taste of the acorn. Such skills have all but disappeared today, but it remains important to realize that wood comes from a living source and is potentially infinitely variable. Working with wood demands at least some knowledge of the characteristics of different species, which may vary not only in general appearance, but also in ease of working, density and texture.

At the same time, it is important to bear in mind that wood products come in varying degrees of authenticity. Solid boards or chunks of timber are self-evidently the real thing, through and through; at the other end of the spectrum, some manufactured 'wood effect' floors or panels may actually contain very little wood at all. They are simply a thin veneer laminated onto a base. In the most synthetic versions of all, paper printed with a wood-like pattern replaces the veneer.

Solid timber is worked in various ways, which determines its appearance and occasionally its durability. Timber which has been cut in a parallel fashion along the length of the log is called plain sawn. This method of working reveals the full rustic character of wood, with knots (a knot marks the beginning of a branch), marks and other variations of colour and pattern. Quarter-sawn wood, where the timber is cut radially, usually results in wood of a more even texture and uniform colour. End-grain, where timber is cut across the grain, is the hardest and most durable of all. Timber suppliers often grade wood according to appearance, with the best or most select grades being those which are largely free of defects. These come mainly from the heartwood, or central portion.

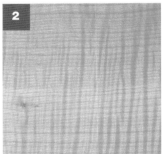

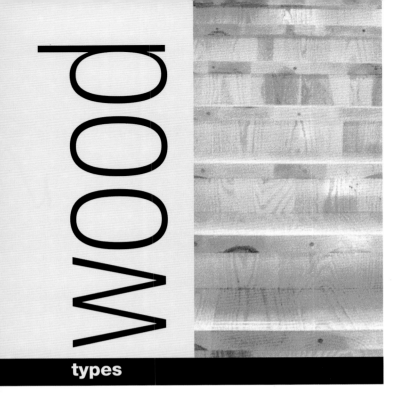

Wood is an incredibly varied material. Types include: plain ash (1), 'quilted' ash veneer (2), white beech (3), cedar of Lebanon (4), American cherry (5), European cherry (6), chestnut (7).

Softwoods and hardwoods

There are some 40,000 known species of trees, but of these less than thirty are in common use. In broad terms, timber species may be roughly divided into two groups: softwoods and hardwoods.

Softwoods generally grow in the colder regions of the world, in the northern American states, Canada, Russia and other parts of the former Soviet Union, and in Scandinavia. Most are evergreen with thin, needle-like leaves and are relatively quick-growing. As a group, softwoods are fairly homogenous. They are typically pale in colour, soft and close-grained, and often 'knotty'. Softwoods comprise various species of pine and deal, including redwood, Scots pine, Norway spruce and white deal.

Softwood is a basic constructional material, and as such it is widely available pre-cut – or 'dimensioned' – to size. The relative softness of these species, together with the presence of resinous knots, makes them less durable than many types of hardwood. Softwoods are generally much cheaper than hardwoods; the best grades are those with the straightest grain and fewest knots. Softwoods must be treated against rot and woodworm before use.

Hardwoods, as a group, are much more varied than softwoods. They grow in both temperate and tropical areas of the world, may be deciduous or evergreen and comprise a wide range of species that differ spectacularly in colour and texture. Most are much more expensive than softwoods and they are generally less readily available. Many species are in serious decline worldwide.

opposite **The lively pattern of grain, as displayed in this staircase, gives wood a sense of vitality.**

above **A custom-made wooden cabinet has exquisite detailing and veneering.**

Throughout history, hardwoods have been prized for their beauty, strength, durability and resistance to pests, or for the ease with which they could be carved.

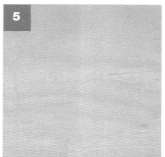

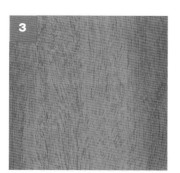
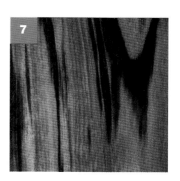
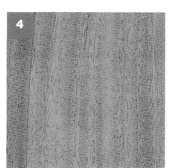
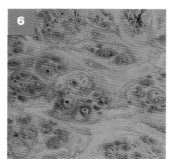

Patterns of grain as well as colour can be very distinctive: sweet chestnut (1), elm (2), Brazilian mahogany (3), African mahogany (4), maple (5), burr maple (6), moera (7).

Seasoning

Like many materials that originate from a living source, wood contains a high percentage of water, varying from softwoods to hardwoods and from one species to the next. Once a tree is felled, it begins to lose moisture at a rate dependent on the surrounding warmth and humidity. This 'seasoning' continues until the timber has acclimatized to its immediate environment, but it never entirely stops.

During seasoning, wood moves, contracting very slightly along the length, but to a much greater extent across the width. This has an obvious impact on dimensions. If 'green' or unseasoned wood were to be used to lay a floor, for example, within a short space of time the boards would have shrunk considerably, perhaps warping and splitting in the process. For this reason, all new timber must be properly seasoned before use. Artificial seasoning in kilns or dehumidifiers is commonly used by commercial timber suppliers to control the seasoning process, drying out the wood at an even, gentle rate to avoid the risk of warping, splitting and distortion. Some suppliers use a combination of natural and artificial drying. Most commercially available timber for interior use is dried to a moisture content of around 10 percent, which is the level recommended for use in centrally heated environments.

Even seasoned wood, however, is sensitive to changes of temperature and humidity. It may be necessary to store wood for a period of time in the room where it will eventually be used so that the timber can further adjust to atmospheric conditions.

Common commercial woods

Ash is widely used in furniture-making and as flooring. It has a straight grain and fairly coarse texture and is tough enough for all-purpose use. The paler shades of cream and biscuit are most typical, but some varieties are darker.

Bamboo is strictly speaking a woody grass, not a true wood, but it is currently finding favour as an environmentally acceptable alternative to hardwood. The plant is the fastest growing in the world and the canes are sufficiently woody and hard to be harvested after only five years. Bamboo boards are made of layers of bamboo strips, laminated under high pressure. Flat-pressing produces boards with a nodular pattern; side-pressing produces boards with a narrower striping of canes. Bamboo flooring is stronger than oak, maple or beech and is very stable. Bamboo panels are also available as wall cladding.

Beech is a popular wood in contemporary design, both for furniture, worksurface and flooring applications. Warm and light in colour, it is very durable and can be even stronger than oak when it is dried under pressure.

Birch is not particularly strong and is commonly used as a facing for plywood. It is pale and fine-grained.

Cedar of Lebanon is an aromatic softwood with a mellow reddish colour and a resistance to pests. Because it acts as a natural moth-repellent, it has commonly been used to make drawer linings, linen cupboards and chests. Commercial cedar, which derives from

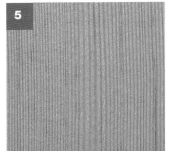

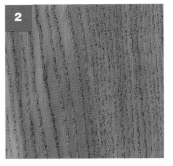

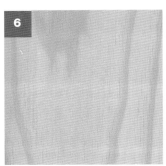
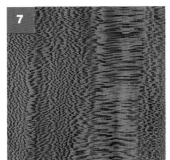

More types of wood: European oak (1), brown oak (2), American red oak (3), padouk (4), British Columbian pine (5), Baltic pine (6), plane lacewood veneer (7).

another type of conifer, is widely used to make shingles and tongue-and-groove panelling.

Cherry has a fine grain and a rich, rosy colour. It is often used as a flooring material or to make a contrasting border.

Chestnut is a strong, durable wood available in a number of different varieties.

Ebony is one of the hardest of all hardwoods. It is characteristically very dense, fine-grained and near-black in colour.

Elm is generally a very strong timber, with a grain that varies from straight to wavy or 'wild'. Colours vary enormously, from creams to rich greenish or purplish browns.

Iroko is an African hardwood very similar in appearance and performance to teak. It is an endangered wood.

Mahogany is a dark, richly coloured tropical hardwood that is fine-grained, naturally resistant to woodworm, strong and easy to carve. Mahogany first appeared in Europe as ballast on ships returning from the West Indian colonies. By the beginning of the eighteenth century, it was beginning to supplant walnut as the furniture-maker's preferred material. Today, mahogany is still in demand for flooring, decorative uses and to make interior features such as doors. It is an endangered wood.

Maple is a near-white wood. It is exceptionally durable and resistant to wear and, as a consequence, is often used as a flooring material in situations where there is heavy traffic, such as in schools and museums.

above **Ecologically sound bamboo makes distinctive wall cladding.**

Oak, once plentiful in northern Europe, is very hard, durable and long-lasting. It can readily be cleft (split along its grain), but it is not particularly easy to work or carve. Its grain is rather open and coarse; with time and weathering, it mellows from pale or mid-brown to a velvety grey. Varieties include English, French and American oak.

Pine, a generic term for many types of softwood, is pale in tone, acquiring a characteristically honey colour when sealed. Widely used in construction, it is one of the most economic types of wood. 'Knotty pine', favoured for wood panelling, is a type of redwood.

Teak is a very durable tropical hardwood with a high degree of weather resistance. A staple constructional material in the East, teak was much associated with Scandinavian furniture design in the post-war period. Other uses include decking and garden furniture. It is an endangered wood.

Walnut is a wood of immense beauty, traditionally highly valued for its rich colour and wavy grain. It is not particularly strong, however, and is prey to woodworm. In the past, walnut was most commonly used as a veneer in furniture-making. American walnut is often used as flooring.

European walnut (1), African walnut (2), American walnut (3), teak (4), wenge (5). Wherever possible, avoid using endangered woods such as mahogany, teak, wenge and padouk.

Wenge is a dark African hardwood, now often associated with fusion styles of decoration.

Exotic timbers include karri, wandu, jarrah, merbau, sucupira, panga panga, padouk, moera, mutenye, lapacho, incienso and jatoba. Many of these species are strikingly coloured and grained.

Antique and reclaimed wood

The dwindling stocks of hardwood, together with an increasing appreciation for the mellowed or distressed quality of time-worn natural materials, have resulted in a thriving market in antique and reclaimed wood. Wood has always lent itself to re-use; in days gone by, salvaged ship's timber was often used to make the stout oak mantel beams in country cottages. Properly maintained, wood – particularly the more durable hardwoods such as oak – can last a very long time, acquiring a beautiful depth of character in the process.

Reclaimed wood ranges from extremely upmarket antique panelling, parquet, floorboards and strip flooring, salvaged from museums, banks and other public buildings, to the humble railway sleeper or scaffolding board. Traditional reclaimed floorboards are generally longer and wider than new boards and are usually made of pine, although hardwoods are also available. Old strip flooring is more likely to be a hardwood. Reclaimed boards are de-nailed and re-machined in such a way as to retain the original surface, but some reclaimed flooring is actually cut from antique beams, old

above **French parquet is acknowledged to be the finest in the world.**

shelving, structural timbers or other similar sources.

Reclaimed parquet is available in a wide range of woods, including oak, maple, Douglas fir and teak. Prices range from comparable to or slightly cheaper than new to extremely expensive, depending on quality and provenance. (French parquet is often of extremely high quality and so is expensive.)

More rough-and-ready effects can be achieved with salvaged timber such as scaffolding planks or railway sleepers (these are

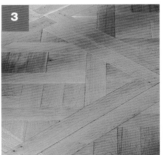

Reclaimed or antique wood has a beautiful patina. Sources include salvage yards and specialist suppliers. Reclaimed iroko (1), limed boards (2), French hardwood parquet (3), oak parquet (4), Oregon pine (5) and wide nineteenth-century pine boards (6) can all be found.

above **A reclaimed railway sleeper has been transformed into a low table.**

blocks may still retain their original hardwood strip or parquet floors. Wooden shutters and panelling, solid or panelled wooden doors and interior mouldings are other common wooden architectural features. Restoring such surfaces involves stripping away old, clogging layers of paint and varnish, either chemically or with a sander; patching and filling may also be required.

Manufactured woods

Man-made boards have a wide range of uses in the building industry, as cladding, sub-floors, panelling, shelving, interior finishes and trim. These materials are generally available in larger sheets and panels than solid timber or boards and they are not as susceptible to changes in humidity or temperature. In recent years, manufactured wood products such as plywood have increasingly been seen as final finishes in their own right. Compared with solid wood, manufactured woods are considerably cheaper.

excellent for use as outdoor flooring or as the vertical surface of raised garden beds).

When sourcing old wood, particularly at the lower end of the market, make sure that it is rot- and pest-free, or you may be importing trouble into your home.

Of course, reclamation can begin at home. Many houses that date from the nineteenth century or earlier have original timber floorboards, at the very least on the upper storeys. Older apartment

Blockboard consists of a core of solid blocks of wood sandwiched between veneers. It comes in a similar range of thicknesses and facing veneers as plywood (see below), but its cut edges may show gaps where the blocks of wood do not meet, so these are therefore generally covered up. Blockboard is cheaper than plywood and tends to be used for shelving light loads.

Cork is derived from the bark of the cork oak, an evergreen native to

Manufactured woods are cheap, utilitarian products that vary in strength and composition. Types include blockboard (1), chipboard (2), MDF (3), thin ply (4) and thick ply (5).

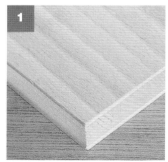

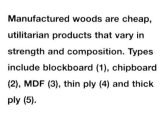

above **Wood laminate flooring is a popular alternative to solid wood.**

Mediterranean regions. It is a relatively cheap material with both many admirable practical qualities and something of an image problem. It is natural in origin, although not entirely in manufacture: to make tiles and sheet, the bark is granulated, mixed with resins, pressed and baked. The process of stripping the bark from the tree does no lasting damage, as the tree simply grows more.

Cork is typically available in tiles of varying thicknesses, grades and dimensions. Flooring-grade cork is harder wearing than the tiles produced as wall covering. One of the most notable characteristics of the material is its springy resilience, which makes it a very comfortable and quiet surface. Colours are generally the natural shades of caramel and honey, but some darker tones are also

available. The major drawback of cork is that it can quickly wear if dirt becomes ingrained, which means that repeat sealing, particularly for cork floors, is essential.

Chipboard is among the cheapest of all manufactured wood products. It consists of chips or fragments of wood bonded with plastic glue and is available ready veneered. It is much weaker than blockboard or plywood and cut edges must not be left exposed as they absorb water readily.

Hardboard is a type of fibreboard in which the fragments of wood are bonded by heat and pressure, not by glue or resin. A relatively thin material, with one rough face and one smooth, it is commonly used as a sub-floor in order to level surface unevennesses.

Medium density fibreboard (MDF) is a relatively new type of wood product, made from tiny particles of wood bonded with plastic resin. An overnight success due to its uniformity, dimensional stability and strength, MDF has a wide variety of uses ranging from shelving and interior trim and mouldings to drawer fronts and cupboard doors. Smooth and sleek once painted or lacquered, MDF is the perfect material for clean-lined contemporary interiors or for creating a seamless look for built-in storage.

Recently, however, questions have been raised both about the material's safety and its environmental impact. Sawing and working MDF inevitably releases a fine chemically impregnated dust which is thought to be injurious to health when inhaled. People working with the material are recommended to wear masks.

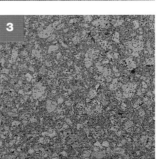

Cork is an environmentally friendly material made from the bark of the cork oak. It is available in different thicknesses and grades, as well as a range of colours: natural (1), dark-stained (2), green (3) and white (4).

above **These chairs are the classic 1946 LCW design by the husband and wife team of Charles and Ray Eames.**

Plywood is a hugely versatile material with a cool, utilitarian aesthetic. Hailed by early modernists as a true machine-age product, laminated bent ply was also much used by designers such as Alvar Aalto to create new expressive furniture forms. Today, plywood still features in many contemporary furniture designs and is also used as a final floor, as well as in a host of behind-the-scenes applications such as sub-floors. Marine ply is used as a sub-floor for mosaic and in areas such as kitchens and bathrooms where moisture occurs.

Plywood is made out of an odd number of thin veneers of wood (known as 'plies') glued together. In most cases, the veneers are laid at right angles to each other, which makes the material equally strong in both directions. A range of thicknesses is also available, with the thinnest being suitable for bending and the thickest being the strongest and most stable.

Different woods are used in the composition of plywood. Among the most common types are birch-faced ply or all-birch ply. North American plywoods are often faced with softwoods such as Douglas fir. Plywood from tropical regions may be faced in a hardwood such as lauan. More expensive plywoods include those which have been faced with an attractive hardwood such as maple, teak or oak.

Wood laminate makes an inexpensive, easy-to-lay flooring. Some laminates are finished with a real wood veneer, while others have a simulated wood finish. Many laminate flooring systems do not require gluing: the sections simply lock together.

Environmental issues

Although wood is theoretically a renewable resource, over recent decades deforestation has become a cause for grave concern. Part of the problem is that current demand far outstrips supply. It is estimated that between 1990 and 1995 alone some 200 million hectares (500 million acres) of forest were lost, an area that is larger than Mexico.

Although media attention has focused on the threat to tropical rainforests particularly in the Amazon Basin and Indonesia, ancient forests worldwide are also in peril, in areas ranging from British Columbia to eastern Russia. Over 80 percent of the world's ancient forests are now believed to have been destroyed; in the United States only 4 percent of 'old-growth' forests remain. These unique habitats, supporting a diverse ecology of plant and wildlife, including trees that may be up to 4,000 years old, are irreplaceable. Many hardwood species from tropical regions are also endangered. These include afromosia, mahogany, teak, iroko, keruing and sapele.

Timber consumption is a major, though not exclusive, cause of deforestation. The sad fact is that much of the timber, whether exotic hardwood or common softwood, is cut to make cheap constructional lumber and plywood simply to supply the voracious demands of the building industry. The result has been the loss of countless species and habitats, increased economic pressure on indigenous communities and a global disaster in the making.

To date, international safeguards have proved patchy and hard to enforce and legislation has done little to prevent the illegal logging that has decimated many forested parts of the globe. Nevertheless, individual consumers can make a considerable impact by ensuring that the timber or timber products they purchase have been produced on a sustainably managed plantation. This is vitally important in the case of exotic or tropical hardwoods. Wood from a socially and environmentally managed forest will bear the symbol of the Forestry Stewardship Council (FSC), an international body that monitors forestry projects worldwide and seeks to balance ecological considerations with the needs of local communities. Similar bodies have had some success in persuading large producers, such as major furniture manufacturers and house-builders, to acquire timber only from approved sources. The international furniture chain IKEA has recently signed up to such a scheme.

wood

however, are those applications where it is the character of the wooden surface that is the point at issue. Applications such as flooring and panelling reveal a positive choice of the material for its own sake.

flooring

Clean-lined but not brutally cutting-edge, expanses of wood flooring have become something of a cliché in contemporary interiors – for good reason. Wood unifies a sequence of spaces but not at the risk of blandness or monotony; it supplies a balanced degree of comfort underfoot whatever the location; and it is available in a wide range of colours, formats and prices. Then there is the 'feel-good factor' that arises from its natural origin, the subtle variety of pattern and grain, the odd creak of a floorboard, the depth of surface that comes from repeated waxing. Wood has its own reticent sensuality which enhances both modern and rustic settings.

Wood flooring has an inherent liveliness that is not simply the result of its surface grain, but also arises from the repeating pattern of the boards. In older terraced or row-house properties, existing timber floors are generally laid at right angles to the underlying flooring joists, which means boards usually run from side wall to side wall, rather than from the front of the house to the back. A new wooden floor, however, can be laid in any direction – down the length of a room to enhance the sense of space, or even diagonally to introduce a different dynamic.

Narrow strip flooring is a popular format, but wide boards, which have a more stately and elegant appearance, are currently the height of fashion. Parquet, short lengths of wood arranged in various patterns, provides the most intricate of all wooden flooring. Common designs are

above **Exposed wooden beams and rafters make an evocative contrast with brickwork walls and an aluminium and wood staircase.**
right **Dark-stained timber framing a waterproof paper Shoji screen suggests an Eastern influence.**

Wood has an immense range of applications. Even in areas of the world where brick or stone are commonly used in house-building, wood still plays an integral role in construction and remains the principal material for a wide range of interior features, uses that range from rafters, flooring joists, the framework of stud walls and staircases, to doors, window frames, mouldings and the carcasses of built-in fittings such as kitchen and vanity units. In many cases, these prosaic uses of wood go largely unseen: wood simply supplies the basis for subsequent decorative or material treatment. Of greater interest in this context,

wood

herringbone and basketweave. At the opposite end of the spectrum, large sheets of ply can make a surprisingly attractive floor and one with a rather seamless quality. Areas of timber decking can extend the use of wooden flooring to outdoor areas.

Like most types of flooring, wood should be laid over a dry, even sub-floor. Existing floorboards levelled with a layer of plywood or hardboard are the optimum surface; if floorboards are not covered, they should be sanded smooth. Wood can also be laid over concrete, provided the sub-floor is covered with a damp-proof membrane and a resilient underlay. The complexity of the work varies, according to the type of flooring. Floors consisting of lengths of solid timber are best fitted professionally; manu-factured strip flooring systems can be installed by a competent amateur.

above **Hardwood decking makes a practical surface for an outdoor terrace and requires little maintenance beyond a yearly scrub.**

left **Wood can be finished in a wide variety of ways. High-gloss floor paint is durable and sleek.**

Solid timber floors are fitted either by secret nailing or as a floating floor. In the case of secret nailing, pins are driven diagonally through the side of the board or block into the underlying sub-floor. For floating floors, tongue-and-groove boards are simply slotted together and fixed only around the perimeter. Certain types of wooden flooring, such as wood block, can be laid with a proprietary adhesive. In all cases, a margin should be left around the edge of the floor to allow for subsequent expansion during periods of high humidity; a gap of about 1.5cm (½ in) is recommended. This gap can be disguised by covering with a shaped wooden moulding.

Wood often forms the unremarkable standard riser and tread format of staircase construction. More evocative are cantilevered planks of solid wood invisibly

left **Clean-lined without being clinical, plywood panels work well in modern settings. Plywood is among the cheapest of all types of wood but makes a surprisingly durable floor.**

above **A beautifully detailed contemporary wooden staircase supported on a steel framework makes a stunning focal point.**

right **Flooring in oiled American walnut provides a rich, dark complement to the black Welsh slate worktop.**

wood

above **The worktop on this island unit is made of solid timber, with inset drainage grooves. The extra thickness of the counter provides a sense of both stability and luxury.**

below **Wood is standard in many fitted kitchens, but here it has been given a new twist. Maple unites upper and lower laminated units, making a splashback, counter, and surface for downlighters.**

supported on metal rods fixed into the wall or similar designs featuring open flights of steps minimally carried on a metal frame.

worksurfaces

Wood makes an ideal material for worksurfaces and countertops, in kitchens, bathrooms and home offices. Durable, reasonably wear-resistant and easy to install, its high degree of practicality is matched by its good looks.

Solid wood worktops are generally made from the heartwood of hardwoods such as beech and oak and come in a range of colours from pale tones through to rich, warm shades. To achieve the desired width, individual sections or 'staves' of wood are jointed together; many suppliers offer a range of pre-cut sizes. The standard thickness is a little over 2.5cm (1in); some tops are available that are twice as thick and look more luxurious. Special mouldings are available that provide a neat finish at junctions with walls and cupboards.

Solid wood worktops are supplied either lacquered or finished with oil. Oil finishing, which preserves the lustrous appearance of the wood, results in a hard, water-repellent surface that resists staining. Nevertheless, prolonged exposure to water should be avoided.

above **Narrow planks are used to clad the walls and ceiling planes of this timber-frame structure. The limewash finish creates an airy, almost nautical feel.**

panelling and cladding

Walls lined in wood have a long history. When European timber stocks were plentiful and cheap, panelling was the most common wall finish in the domestic interior. Panelling bare stone or brick walls in wood provided an obvious and effective means of insulation against cold and damp, but it also served to create a sense of psychological warmth and comfort, qualities no less desirable today.

Early panelling consisted of fairly small, thin panels framed by vertical stiles and horizontal rails which were plugged into the wall. Up until the eighteenth century, most panelling was made of oak or some other hardwood. Decorative embellishment might have taken the form of linenfold carving, simulating the rippled surface of draped fabric; painted treatments were also common. By the eighteenth century, softwood had become the principal material. Panelling was now designed to conform with classical proportions, dividing walls in the familiar divisions of cornice, dado and skirting. Later, under the influence of Rococo, wall panels became more curved and fluid in outline.

At the same time, a much simpler style of panelling continued to be popular in rustic areas. Match-boarding or tongue-and-groove panelling, as it is known today, comprised plain planks of softwood framed by posts: it was used as a practical means of covering walls and ceilings and was

wood

generally painted. In ordinary nineteenth-century households, the lower portion or dado of walls in service areas and corridors was often treated in this fashion as a way of resisting wear and tear.

Historic styles of panelling inevitably give any interior a period feel. A panelled room is also a fitted room, snug and enclosed: the traditional country house library or study are obvious points of reference. Eighteenth- or early nineteenth-century-style panelled room schemes, in woods such as pine, cherry, ash, mahogany or oak, can be commissioned from specialist firms and may be designed to incorporate built-in features such as fire surrounds, cupboards, bookcases and niches. Needless to say, such schemes are very expensive; the result may well be more reminiscent of corporate boardroom than country rectory.

Simpler panelling styles have a greater

left **Svelte plywood panels provide a subtle tactile background in the home of a fashion designer.**

below **Walls clad in bamboo, notched and framed to cover walls and doors, have a pleasing rippling texture that is set off by the black-stained timber flooring.**

above **Waney-edged rough timber planks angled at a window create an unusual louvred screen that filters the light.**

below **This loft conversion features original exposed timbers and large panels of utilitarian chipboard.**

degree of versatility in the contemporary home. Most popular is tongue-and-groove boarding, widely available in kit form as a means of cladding dados or of providing a unified surface in fitted areas such as bathrooms. Such wood cladding is best painted, leaving the rhythm of the boarding to suggest a 'woody' effect. While other types of panelling are also available off-the-peg and can be readily installed by a competent amateur, true panelling is always jointed rather than fixed, so that moisture movement can be accommodated. This is best commissioned from a craftsman specializing in the work.

Knotty pine, either planked or panelled, is a popular interior finish in American homes, particularly for studies and family or recreation rooms. Made of redwood, the rich warm colour and rustic overtones of this simple finish give interiors an unpretentious, down-to-earth quality; sound insulation is a plus, too, in rooms devoted to entertainment and relaxation.

Sheets of wood – particularly ply faced with an attractive hardwood – can be used to pick out a plane of wall in the same sort of manner as a splash of strong colour. The material contrast between plaster and wood adds a certain depth of character, a textural change of pace. This type of treatment is particularly effective when it serves to define room arrangement or an area of activity within a multi-purpose space – on a wall

flanking a dining area, for example, or as a type of extended bedhead. Full-height sliding wooden panels provide another variation on the same theme, screening built-in storage or serving as flexible room dividers.

fittings and features

Wood serves as the workhorse material of a wide variety of fitted elements, including shelving, kitchen units, vanity units and built-in storage of all kinds. There is a vast range in terms of quality and price, from bespoke kitchens entirely fitted out in solid oak to cheap and cheerful flat-pack units thinly veneered in birch or beech.

In these essentially practical contexts, wood is almost a victim of its own success. Sheer familiarity means that its particular qualities cease to register. But a little lateral thinking can serve to redress the balance. Most wooden shelving tends to be fairly

applications

above **A trough-like sink made of solid teak is reminiscent of the traditional Japanese hot tub. Such fittings must be expertly constructed to prevent leakage.**

right **Natural, unprocessed timber has a raw appeal. Here, a table constructed of rough planks is supported by a framework of metal scaffolding.**

opposite, above **Narrow strips of solid hardwood have been used to follow the contours of the bath.**

opposite, below **These niches have been neatly lined in warm wood veneer and downlit to enhance the display of decorative objects.**

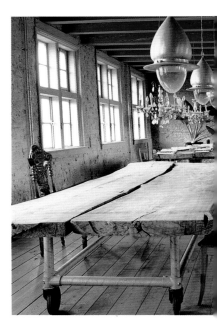

reticent in terms of design and is often painted in with the main wall colour. Thick cantilevered wooden shelves widely spaced give the material a greater prominence; another alternative is to employ waney-edged wood (timber which retains a raw bark edge) or to make use of distressed or salvaged boards. In a similar way, stools, table tops and benches made of rough-hewn chunks of wood or reclaimed boards or sleepers restore a more elemental quality to the use of the material. 'Poor' types of wood, such as plywood, have a similar utilitarian aesthetic.

A less expected use of wood is to make handbasins and baths. Japanese-style hot tubs have been a notable accompaniment to minimalist design: these are most effective and practical when used merely for soaking (in the East, one washes first under running water and gets into the tub clean in order to relax). The optimum material is aromatic (and antibacterial) cedarwood; some tubs and basins are made in beech, wenge or birch. These tend to be expensive fittings and are available from a number of specialist suppliers; if you commission a tub from a cabinet maker, make sure that it is properly jointed and finished so that it does not leak. Wooden tubs need to be regularly filled with water to prevent the wood drying out and splitting.

finishes

The beauty of wood lies in the liveliness of its surface, its pattern of graining and natural, warm tones. Obviously, wood can be covered up with paint – historically the correct treatment for softwood features and fittings – but finishes which enhance the intrinsic character of the material are generally more satisfying. Good quality hardwood really needs no subsequent treatment bar protective sealing (see **Care and Maintenance** below). In the case of softwoods, however, lightening or darkening

the wood extends the decorative range.

'Limed' or 'pickled' finishes bleach out natural wood tones, simulating weathering and age. Pale pickled wood, notably oak, was particularly associated with the luxurious style of society decorators such as Syrie Maugham and Elsie de Wolfe in the early decades of the twentieth century; nowadays, however, liming has become a popular way of toning down the sometimes strident orange tones of pine. Proprietary liming wax or some other form of white pigment is rubbed into the grain of the wood to create the desired effect.

Because of its absorbency, wood also lends itself to staining. A wide range of wood stains are available, both water- and spirit-based, and in innumerable shades from woody tones to primaries. The

applications

left **Herringbone parquet introduces a strong sense of rhythm to a pared-down contemporary interior.**

right **Wooden stairs, timber panelling and fretwork balustrading painted a matt, chalky white have an appealing rustic simplicity in this eighteenth-century Swedish country house.**

wood

advantage of stain over paint as a finish is that the pattern of the grain remains visible. Staining ordinary softwood a dark colour suggests the richness of hardwood.

care and maintenance

Wood requires a certain amount of upkeep to remain in good condition. The main enemy is damp, which in extreme conditions can lead to various forms of rot and decay. Sealing with a proprietary wood seal, or with oil and wax, is essential to prevent moisture from penetrating the surface and serves as a barrier to both chemical attack and staining.

Many wooden floors are supplied ready sealed and require little in the way of further maintenance. The traditional finish for hardwood is tung oil. After fitting, oil-finished floors should be coated with wax which will buff up to a soft sheen and resist scratches. Waxing should be repeated every six months to a year, depending on the wear that the floor receives. For floors that are subject to heavier traffic or those that are laid in humid environments such as kitchens and bathrooms, a lacquered finish provides a high degree of protection and should last for years.

Wood that is not supplied ready-finished – as well as old wood which has been sanded – will require several coats of seal once in situ, and possibly subsequent waxing. Seals take a certain amount of time to cure; you may need to sand the surface lightly between coats. There are a wide variety of types of seal on the market, which vary in composition, longevity and appearance. Before you apply a seal to a floor or other wood surface, test it out to assess its effect on tone and texture. Plywood and cork should also be sealed.

Many commonly available wood seals contain polyurethane, which has a yellowish

above **Pale wood flooring maximizes the light under the eaves in an attic bedroom. The sloping ceiling is clad in plywood panels.**

tinge and tends to yellow further with age; it can also irritate the eyes and skin. All seals which are solvent- rather than water-based are flammable and potentially toxic and should be applied with care: keep rooms well ventilated and wear gloves and a protective face mask.

Non-toxic alternatives include acrylic varnish, which is water-based, and various types of 'natural' or environmentally friendly products. These finishes are generally not as hard-wearing and many require waxing up to three or four times a year.

Once finished, wooden surfaces should be dusted, swept or vacuumed at regular intervals to prevent a build-up of dirt and grit which can penetrate the finish and allow water through. Special mild soapy cleaners which do not require rinsing are available.

Aside from the wear and tear of regular traffic, wood is particularly susceptible to damage from stiletto heels and furniture legs. High heels will quickly pockmark a floor, particularly if it is made of softwood, breaking through a sealed finish and letting

in dirt and moisture. Occasionally, a small area of damage can be resanded and patched with seal, but a badly worn floor will require a complete overhaul. Bear in mind, however, that some types of cheaper wood flooring, which consist of only a thin veneer over a composition wood base, cannot be sanded.

If you are looking for a completely maintenance-free wood floor, however, manufactured strips may be the answer. These high-pressure laminates require little upkeep beyond routine sweeping and will resist almost any kind of damage, including that caused by high heels, heavy furniture, and cigarette burns. These high levels of performance are achieved at the cost of authenticity: such products are only nominally 'wood' and may look it.

Wooden worktops require very little maintenance aside from wiping over with a clean, damp cloth. Minor scratching can be removed by applying a thin coat of proprietary oil; badly marked surfaces may need resanding and finishing.

stone

left **Stone flooring introduces a sense of permanence to the interior. The matt surface of dark granite on this stairway has a timeless appeal.**

right **Beautiful Portuguese limestone used for flooring throughout this property looks coolly contemporary and luxurious. The space-saving 'paddle' steps have limestone treads.**

Stone endures. It has weight and presence; its monumental quality and sense of timelessness lend permanence to the interior. Designing with stone makes a statement about staying power: this is not a quick-fix material for a cosmetic revamp, but one which integrates structure with surface at the most fundamental level.

It is not necessary to have a thorough appreciation of the finer points of geology to appreciate that stone owes its unique qualities to its origin as the very bedrock of the earth. Some types of stone are younger than others, but all date back millions of years to the titanic processes that led to the formation of the earth's crust. These ancient beginnings, when molten lava streams cooled, rivers and seas laid down their sediments, and intense heat and pressure fractured and crystallized rock, remain visible in the rich character and patterning of different types of stone.

Like any natural material, stone is subject to wear and decay; unlike most, however, significant deterioration is measured on a very long timescale indeed. It takes centuries of footfalls and scrubbing to erode even the softest stone floor appreciably. From a human perspective, stone appears as immutable as a material can be, which is one reason why it is the material that has been most commonly used throughout history to build sacred monuments, from

pyramids and monolithic standing stone circles, to Greek temples and medieval cathedrals with their fine Gothic tracery. Some architectural critics have gone so far as to suggest that the spiritual centres of civilizations have typically been founded where there was a convenient outcrop of rock that could be employed to give eternal expression to religious ideals.

At the same time, the inherent strength of stone and the fact that it is not readily damaged by fire or attack has also led to its use in many different types of fortified building, such as castles, garrisons, forts and strongholds. Because stone is capable of withstanding very great loads, both secular and sacred stone structures could also be much larger than buildings made of other materials.

Stone is found all over the world, but it is not readily or uniformly available in all localities. In Britain, where a wide variety of different types of stone are found in fairly close proximity to one another, stone has long been a feature of vernacular or domestic buildings, such as cottages, barns and farmhouses. If one were to plot those English towns and villages where limestone buildings are most common, for example, the result would be a fairly accurate map of the

left **Irregular stone flags make a feature floor in a living area, effectively contrasting with hardwood flooring in adjacent areas.**

belt of limestone deposits, a narrow curving band that begins around Portland Bill and sweeps up through the Cotswolds to the Humber and the Cleveland Hills of Yorkshire. This convergence is far from surprising when one realizes that transporting stone often cost more than the material itself.

Quarrying, transporting and working stone has always been a slow, costly, labour-intensive process, and one that has not appreciably improved since mechanization. Relatively unfinished stone, such as freestone or fieldstone cleared from the land, is a feature of the construction of humble buildings the world over; in finer surroundings, however, the presence of stone cut and dressed for a precision fit, or intricately and painstakingly sculpted, is redolent of wealth and prestige. Stone was particularly prized in the eighteenth century, both for its classical associations and as an emblem of status. At this time, it was far from uncommon for existing brick houses to be clad or faced in stone as a form of architectural and social elevation; while, more economically, humbler materials such as cement, stucco and plaster were also widely employed to create the 'effect' of stone.

From this history of use have come stone's varied cultural associations: rugged and rustic; noble, sacred and refined. One of the many beauties of stone is this richness of meaning: whatever you want to say, there is a type of stone to say it for you. Riven slate or Yorkstone flags have the down-to-earth appeal of a country rectory or farmhouse; polished marble is classically luxurious; pale, cool limestone has a reticent contemporary edge. Few natural materials are available in such a stunning variety of colours and surface patterning. The popular image of stone as pale and matt is belied by a range of shades that includes black, blue, purple, orange, green, flame-red and golden yellow; by textures that may be pitted, honed, sandy or smooth as glass; and by mottled, striated, flecked, veined or crystalline patterns. Many of these associative and aesthetic qualities can be heightened when stone is used in sympathetic combination with other materials such as wood, glass and metal.

left **A black granite basin and shelf add a sense of presence to a bathroom. The door is in sandblasted glass.**

right **Slate, with its dark tones and sleek 'wet' look, makes an evocative backdrop for a wetroom floored in teak and tiled in green ceramic tiles.**

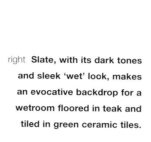

Aside from its use as a constructional material, stone has a wide range of applications in the interior. Although the most common is flooring – including stairs and outdoor paving – stone is increasingly employed as a cladding or tiling material for walls or fire surrounds and in the form of kitchen countertops and worksurfaces. One of the most expressive (and indulgent) use of the material is to create baths and basins. As with most materials, particular types of stone are better suited to certain uses than others, depending on porosity, wear-resistance and surface texture. Another important element to consider is lateral strength. Slate, for example, which has a high degree of lateral strength, performs more reliably as stair treads than crystalline materials such as marble, which crack more readily.

Stone's obvious practical characteristics include hardness, coldness and heaviness. As a hard, unyielding material, it has a tendency to amplify sound; as a floor, it is implacably ungiving and multiplies the likelihood of accidental breakages. Stone's coolness, a welcome factor in warm climates, may prove less of an advantage in more temperate parts of the world. And its heaviness means that some on-site investigation may well be required before it is installed, to ensure that sub-structures, supporting frameworks or sub-floors can bear the weight. Despite its image of immutability, stone is not maintenance-free; many types require sealing and cleaning with specialist solvents or soaps.

A significant factor in the use of the material remains its expense. Stone is never a cheap option. The price of stone varies from fairly expensive to astronomical, according to type, and, while reclaimed or salvaged stone can occasionally be an economical choice, some antique pavers or tiles are even more costly than new ones. Added to the price of the material is the cost of installation, which can in some cases be almost as much again. Laying or installing stone is not a job for an amateur: an experienced professional will ensure that the quality of the material is not compromised.

Stone demands a certain commitment. But, in exchange, the right choice of stone in the right situation delivers a profound sense of continuity, a timeless quality that is beyond fashion, beyond even history, that stretches right back to the origins of the earth itself.

stone
types

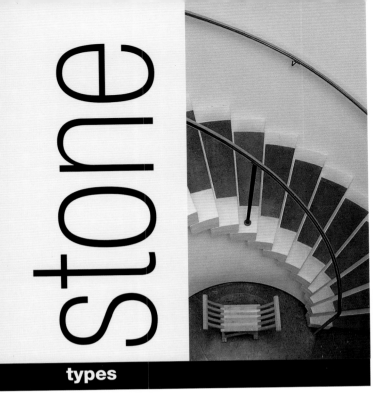

above **Slate inset treads lend graphic contrast to a curved concrete staircase.**

Stone comes in an impressive variety of types, colours, patterns and surface textures, from sources all over the world. Broadly speaking, all varieties of stone fall into three main categories: igneous, sedimentary and metamorphic. These classifications correspond to the methods of formation.

Igneous rock comprises the oldest types of stone, those formed during the cooling of the earth's crust thousands of millions of years ago. As the magma or molten rock cooled, it crystallized, giving these types of stone a typically granular appearance. Granite, which originated deep within the earth, is an igneous rock; basalt, which is finer-grained, is lava that solidified once it reached the surface. Igneous rocks are exceptionally dense, which means that they are both very wear-resistant and capable of taking a high polish.

Sedimentary rocks derive from more recent geological periods and are the result of the consolidation of various forms of deposits laid down in strata by rivers, lakes, seas, ice, or by precipitation. Sandstone is a type of sedimentary rock composed of fragments of other rocks and minerals compressed and cemented together. Limestones, which are also sedimentary rocks, were formed in two

principal ways. The most common type of limestone – organic limestone – is composed of the shells, skeletons and secretions of marine creatures including molluscs and corals, together with plant material; the other type – inorganic – is the result of precipitation from solutions of carbonates. Sedimentary rock is much softer than igneous rock.

The final, and most recent, category is metamorphic rock. Metamorphic rock is rock that has been subjected to intense heat and pressure during the movement of the earth's crust and the formation of mountain ranges. Marble, a metamorphic rock, derives from recrystallized limestone and dolomite. Slate, another type, is exceptionally hard.

These broad categories of stone, which superficially seem so clearcut, demand a certain degree of qualification. To begin with, many types of stone are commonly – and confusingly – named after the places where they are found, which can obscure their geological classification. But not all types of stone are precisely geologically distinguishable from one another: limestones and sandstones, for example, often share many characteristics. Stone, even of the same type, varies according to locality: no two quarries are alike. At the same time, stones from the same quarry also vary. The diversity of the material serves as a constant reminder of its natural origin.

below **Large-scale limestone tiles bring a sense of visual unity to the walls, floor and bath in a small space.**

Granite

Incredibly strong, dense and hard, granite is the toughest of all types of stone. Quarried all over the world, it is typically found in mountain regions in Norway, France, Scotland, Devon and Cornwall, Wales, Ireland, eastern Canada and the northeastern United States. It has an even, grainy texture that is capable of taking a high polish and does not display any appreciable patina after wear or weathering. Granite is virtually impregnable, resistant to air pollution and impervious to water – all strong practical reasons why it has been commonly used for areas of heavy public traffic, such as for kerbstones and pavers.

The mottled, crystalline appearance of granite derives from the presence of the minerals felspar, mica and quartz, with felspar contributing the typical pink, grey and red colours, and mica lending glitter and sparkle. The relatively even patterning of the stone can make it look relentless if used extensively. Granite-built towns such as Aberdeen or Rennes in Brittany display this rather dour quality. But in smaller doses and more vivid colours, it can be used to give a graphic counterpoint to an interior scheme.

Granite for interior domestic use is available in the form of tiles of varying dimensions and thicknesses for flooring or cladding walls, or as solid slabs for worksurfaces and countertops. Individual

above **Honed granite is an ideal choice if a warm look is required.**

granite blocks or rough-textured setts, similar to those used in outdoor spaces, are more practical for flooring applications than highly polished tiles. Granite, particularly in slab form, is very expensive; tiles are a cheaper and less heavy option.

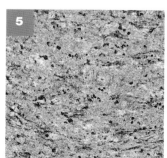

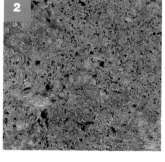

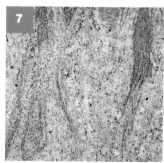

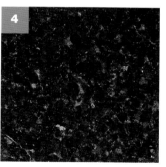

Strong colour and bold flecking are typical characteristics of granite. Shades include near-black (1), blue-grey (2), rich brown (3), deep green (4), pink (5), gold (6) and grey (7).

Marble

A crystallized type of limestone formed by intense heat or pressure, marble is unsurpassed for its translucent beauty. Although marble is found worldwide in mountainous areas, the finest and purest comes from Italy. This comparative rarity, together with the fact that marble is capable of taking a high polish, has long enhanced its desirability.

Pure marble is almost completely white. Colours come from the presence of iron oxides and other mineral deposits – technically impurities – but which give rise to a wide range of shades including green, pink, red, brown, gold and black. Patterning is equally distinctive: fissures and cracks, veining and a soft clouding which gives the stone an impression of depth and translucence.

For centuries the epitome of luxury, marble has something of an image problem today. Long prized for its beauty and used extensively in grand surroundings in the form of floors and staircases, columns, fire surrounds and chimneypieces, marble was an important element of classical eighteenth century architecture, even if the marble halls of English country houses proved a much chillier and less hospitable environment than the Palladian villas of Italy. The extent to which marble was identified with opulence and refinement can be judged from the numerous examples of *faux* marbling in less exalted surroundings.

If the sheer opulence of marble is somewhat at odds with simple, contemporary styles of decorating, marble look-alikes in plastic laminate, linoleum and vinyl have served to debase the material's aesthetic currency. Part of the problem is overfamiliarity; part derives from the fact that many simulated marble finishes are almost as convincing, visually at least, as the real thing. In this context, the use of marble can sometimes seem less a hallmark of refinement and more a case of vulgar indulgence.

With such reservations in mind, marble remains one of the most beautiful of all natural materials; it is also one of the most expensive.

above **Walls clad in marble mosaic complement a marble washbasin.**

Modern methods have resulted in the availability of more economical, thinner and lighter marble tiles – a practical format for flooring or cladding. Highly polished textures are best reserved for counters, wall tiles or vanity tops; a honed or slightly sanded finish makes a more practical surface underfoot.

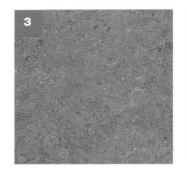

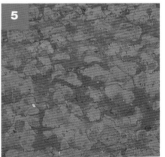

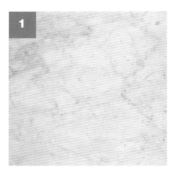

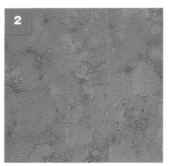

Marble is a supremely luxurious stone, with a price tag to match. Pure white Carrara marble (1) is among the most prized. Other colours include rose (2), dull gold (3), deep green (4) and russet (5).

Slate

One of the most versatile of all types of stone used in construction, slate's unique property is that it can readily be split into thin planes, owing to the way in which its mica content has been transformed by metamorphic processes. This ease of working, and the useful sheet-like format that results, has led to the widespread use of slate as pavers, stairs and steps, roofing tiles, pantry shelves and even water tanks and troughs. On contemporary buildings, slate is often used in the form of exterior facing or cladding panels. Unlike other types of stone, slate is laterally strong, which means that, with proper support, cracking is rarely an issue.

Some of the best slate in the world is generally acknowledged to come from Wales; Devon and Cornwall have also been historically important sources. Slate from Delabole in Cornwall, known as blue-stone, has commonly been used for paving. Other slate regions can be found in North America, Spain, South America, India and Africa.

Available in near-solid shades and mottled or veined patterns, most types of slate have a rather sleek, wet appearance owing to their mica content. Typical colours are the brooding 'slatey' shades of blue-grey and grey-green, along with charcoal black, but Mexican, Indian and African slate is often vividly coloured and patterned.

Slate's versatility as a building material is matched by an equivalent aesthetic range: depending on its surface texture, it can be spare and contemporary, or rustic-looking. In the modern idiom,

above **Riven slate tiles create a cool effect for the walls of a shower.**

slate is available in tiles and slabs and with a smooth, honed finish. Slate that has been split, rather than sawn, is described as 'riven'. Its surface is attractively irregular, with shallow ridges and its edges may also be roughly chipped, which adds to the traditional farmhouse look. Riven slate is generally available in thicker, smaller slabs than sawn varieties: the uneven camber of riven slate must also be accommodated in laying and fixing.

Practically speaking, slate is hard, durable and waterproof, which means that its uses extend to outdoor areas as well. It is cheaper than granite, marble or limestone; most economical of all is reclaimed slate from salvage yards, which can be half the price of new.

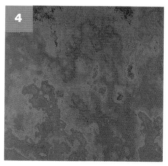

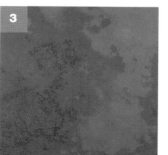

Slate comes in a range of intense, moody colours, with many of the more colourful varieties coming from India. The usual shades are deep blue-black (1), dull purple (2), green (3) and grey-green (4). More exotic are mottled (5) and silvery (6) varieties.

Limestone

Limestone comprises a broad family of different types of stone, which vary significantly in character. Softer than igneous rocks such as granite, limestone nevertheless shares the timeless, rather monumental quality common to all types of stone.

While limestone is quarried all over the world, French varieties are acknowledged to be among the best, being typically very hard and non-porous, and hence highly suitable for paving and flooring.

above **A floor is made of French blue limestone slabs inset with slate 'dots'.**

Chalky or creamy Caen stone is found around Boulogne; other types are quarried in central regions and in the south and west, especially in the hills of Provence. France is also a premier source of antique limestone.

One of the most familiar English varieties of limestone is Bath or Cotswold stone, a warm golden limestone widely used not only in

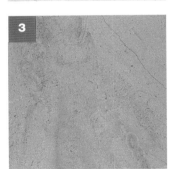

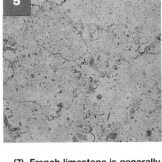

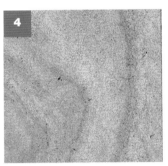

Limestone is typically neutral in tone, ranging from creamy white (2) through to warmer honey or golden shades (3, 4, 5). Most types of limestone reveal some surface flecking, veining or mottling, the trace evidence of marine deposits (1); in some varieties the patterning is particularly marked

(7). French limestone is generally acknowledged to be the highest quality; Portuguese limestone is also sought after. Some of the most expensive limestones are the relatively rare blue or blue-grey varieties (5). Other shades include grey-green (8) and 'bitter chocolate'.

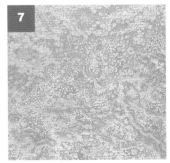

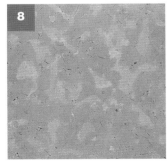

the construction of many Oxford colleges but also in cottages and farmhouses throughout the entire Cotswold area. Other well known types include Portland stone, which is milky white; travertine, quarried in Tuscany, a hard pitted limestone commonly used for paving; and Jerusalem limestone from the Hebron Mountains, which is golden in colour.

Despite its long and distinguished history of use, limestone has a strong contemporary appeal. In part, this is due to its characteristic neutrality: most limestones are light and subtle in tone. Limestone also lacks marble's more conspicuous associations with luxury, a reticence which works well in pure, modern interiors. Cool and elegant, polished limestone can look almost luminous.

Limestone is typically pale in colour, encompassing the narrow spectrum of natural shades from off-white to biscuit to light grey. A few varieties, however, are more intensely coloured; these rarer types include blue, green, bitter chocolate and near-black. Almost all limestone displays some form of subtle patterning in the form of flecks, veins or mottled patches. Its most beguiling feature is fossilized shells or the evidence of ancient marine deposits.

Sandstone

Like limestone, sandstone is also a sedimentary rock but its high quartz content means that it is considerably harder and hence more wear-resistant. As the name suggests, this type of stone is typically sandy both in colour and texture, ranging from pale fawn through to deep reddish brown, but there are also grey varieties. Common sandstone formats include flags and small blocks or 'setts'.

Perhaps the best-known of all sandstones is Yorkstone, which unsurprisingly derives from Yorkshire in England. Because it is frost-resistant, hard-wearing and can be riven to create a ridged, non-slip surface, Yorkstone is particularly appropriate for use outdoors as garden paving. The popularity of Yorkstone, however, is giving cause for concern, and the material is on the verge of becoming rare.

below **Yorkstone is extremely hard-wearing and ages beautifully.**

Sandstone generally wears better than limestone and is available in small setts suitable for outdoor use as well as paving slabs. Colours are typically 'sandy' shades, from pale biscuit to deep reddish brown: sandstones from the south of France (1); the west of England (2) and Tuscany (3).

The effectiveness of a pebble or cobble mosaic depends on colour contrast. The most common stones used for the purpose are made of granite, quartz and limestone, with granite supplying the darker tones in a design, quartz the lighter and limestone the creamy or graduated mid-tones. Pebbles are supplied pre-graded for size.

Pebble and cobble mosaics are best suited for feature areas outdoors, such as paths, focal points or borders. Mosaics comprising smaller pebbles can be used successfully as flooring indoors, but individual stones do have a tendency to work loose.

Antique and distressed stone

All natural materials have the capacity to age with time, acquiring a patina that gives an evocative sense of depth and character. It is hardly surprising that antique stone, worn and softened by the passing of time, should be so highly prized. Because it takes a great many years before most types of stone acquire that mellow quality, the cost of real antique stone can be anything up to double that of newly quarried varieties. Stone reclaimed from derelict monasteries, chateaux and country houses is also in dwindling supply, which only serves to drive prices up further.

above **Whitewashed cobbles make an unusual, tactile floor in a bathroom.**

Pebbles and cobbles

Mosaics composed of pebbles and cobbles have an ancient history, with the oldest known example dating back to Turkey in the eighth-century AD. A common outdoor feature in Mediterranean areas, the technique was subsequently introduced by the Moors to the Iberian Peninsula in the fourteenth century. Today, a number of mosaic artists are working in the discipline, creating original designs to individual specification.

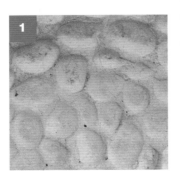

The most expensive types of stone are often antique varieties, reclaimed from churches and old houses (2, 3 and 4). The price reflects the limited supply. Pebble or cobble pavements (1) are best suited to outdoor areas but can find limited applications indoors.

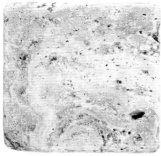

above **Tumbling is a method of artificially distressing stone to suggest the patina of age. These examples are marble.**

For those who desire the look of old stone but cannot afford it, most stone is available with a distressed finish – a treatment that simulates an antique appearance (see Formats and finishes).

Formats and finishes

Stone is heavy, unwieldy and prone to damage in transit, and these factors have a considerable bearing on the formats that are available. The limitations of hand-working meant that in the past stone tended to be supplied in thicker slabs or irregularly shaped flags; today, with modern mechanized processes, tile formats have become much more widely available. Thinner, lighter and easier to install, tiles are suitable for both flooring and cladding purposes. Another advantage of tiles is that they are uniformly dimensioned, which produces a neat, seamless surface. Handworked stone may be preferred for a rustic look.

Stone tiles come in a range of sizes and thicknesses, depending on the type of stone and intended use. Wall tiles may be as thin as 6mm (¼in); flooring tiles range from 1cm (⅜in) to 2cm (¾in) thick, with the larger sizes being thicker of necessity. On the aesthetic side, larger tiles increase the appearance of monumentality and are best suited to greater expanses; small tiles look better in more confined surroundings.

Setts – small rough-textured blocks of stone – are another flooring option. Granite and sandstone setts, widely used in outdoor paving, can also be used in the interior, particularly where robust and non-slip surfaces are desirable.

Worksurfaces, vanity tops and other built-in stone features are generally made from slabs of varying thicknesses. For the thinnest slabs, slate is the stone of choice since granite, limestone and travertine offer little resistance to cracking.

When ordering stone, particularly for flooring or cladding, an allowance must be made for wastage. Even with professional laying or installation, some damage may occur to individual tiles, either in transit or in the process of fitting. Blending is also an issue. Natural stone is not a uniform material and many varieties vary significantly in colour and pattern, from slab to slab or tile to tile. It is advisable to consult suppliers during specification to ensure that stones are as evenly matched as possible; an experienced installer will also be able to make adjustments during fitting so that the overall effect is harmonious and does not display abrupt contrasts.

Textural variation is another significant variable. How a surface feels and performs will depend to a large extent on its finish; different finishes will also affect the visual appearance of the stone.

Stone finishes include honed, polished, sanded, riven and textured. Honed – a matt satiny texture – is smooth and non-reflective and provides friction where stone is to be used for flooring. Polishing provides a highly reflective gloss finish. Only the harder types of stone, such as granite, marble and travertine, will take a high polish. This finish is generally too slippery to be suitable for floors. Sanded finishes are more abrasive and slip-resistant than honed finishes. Riven is a finish unique to slate (see page 55). Textured or distressed finishes – flaming, tumbling, sand-blasting and bush-hammering – bring out the colours and create an impression of weathering. Tumbling blurs and softens hard edges in a way that is suggestive of wear; flaming releases the quartz content of particular types of stone.

Different finishes alter the appearance as well as the texture of stone. Common finishes include sandblasted (a, e), honed (b, h), polished (c), flame-textured (d, f) and sanded (g). Limestone is shown on the right, granite below and slate below right.

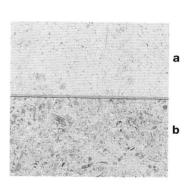
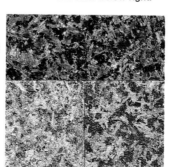
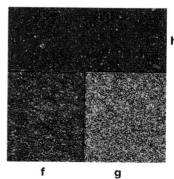

stone

flooring

Stone floors convey a sense of importance and permanence to the interior. Highly suitable for areas in the home which receive heavy traffic, such as hallways, or for kitchens and bathrooms where water resistance is important, stone flooring is also increasingly seen as a treatment for living areas, particularly in contemporary interiors. The inherent chilliness of a stone floor can be mitigated by underfloor heating.

It is also important to choose finishes that provide a degree of friction underfoot and thus avoid excess slipperiness.

The effect of stone flooring can be cool, classic and elegant, or rustic and countrified depending on the type and format of the stone. One classic pattern comprises light-coloured stone octagons (often marble) contrasting with dark cabuchon insets (often slate). But a subtle sense of pattern can also arise simply in the

above **The neat gridded pattern of rectangular slate tiles used both on the walls and floor and set off by white grouting lends a graphic crispness to this interior scheme. Wall cabinets are in maple.**

manner of laying. Staggered courses have a light, open quality; regular grids provide a sense of elegance and order; randomly shaped flagstones are more down-to-earth and informal. Many stone floors are enhanced by contrasting borders which provide additional decorative detail.

Before specifying a stone floor for a particular location, it is essential to establish whether the existing sub-floor will bear the weight. Timber floors on upper levels may

not be strong enough. Stone also requires a perfectly dry, even base that is not prone to movement – any camber or flex in the base floor will lead to cracking. In the case of timber sub-floors, two layers of boarding may need to be applied to reduce the natural 'give', particularly if the floor is suspended. Special board designed as tile backing is advisable, as this resists moisture. Similarly, solid concrete sub-floors should be dry, even and level.

left **Rough and rustic fieldstone walls contrast with vividly veined granite flooring.**

(6½ft) wide, it is usual to allow a flexible joint of between 6mm (¼in) and 1cm (⅜in) around the perimeter of the floor. The thickness of the joints between individual tiles depends on the type of stone. Smooth, regular tiles

Stone can be laid in one of two ways: either in a sand/cement bed or with adhesive. Sand/cement beds are only suitable for concrete or screeded sub-floors. The bed is generally laid thicker than required so that the tiles compact it and prevent air spaces which can cause subsequent cracking. Most stone tiles, however, are now laid with proprietary adhesive, either in a thin bed, in the case of level floors, or in a thicker bed to take up any surface unevenness.

Joints must be incorporated within the stone floor to allow for any future movement caused by heat, changes in humidity or flexing of the sub-floor. For floors over 2m can be laid with narrow joints of between 2mm (¹/₁₆in) and 3mm (⅛in). Riven slate, hand-finished and textured stone tiles, which are less regular in shape, will require wider joints, up to 1cm (⅜in) thick. Grouting should be chosen to match the colour and tone of the stone.

Where stone has been used extensively as a flooring, stone staircases provide visual

above **A floor composed of square tiles of matt Spanish limestone makes a subtle, elegant background. Suede upholstery pursues the textural theme.**

left **Black Brazilian slate flooring sets off walls of textured Japanese plasterwork, finished with a rough raked surface.**

continuity from level to level. In this context, however, certain practicalities assume even greater importance. Slate is perhaps the best choice for staircases, as it has sufficient lateral strength to be used in relatively thin sections and can even be used where the staircase consists of open treads. Granite and limestone, on the other hand, require the support of a staircase framework and need to be used in thicker sections of approximately 3cm (1¼in) to prevent cracking. Special nosings, grooved recesses or anti-slip inserts may be required to provide adequate friction on the stairs.

applications

stone

cladding

Stone provides an elegant alternative to ceramic tiles as a means of cladding wall surfaces in kitchen and bathroom areas. For most interior purposes, stone tiles up to 1.5cm (½ in) can simply be fixed directly to the wall using proprietary adhesive. It is important to ensure that lighter and more porous types of stone, such as limestones, are not stained in the process.

If larger stone panels are required, to face a bath, for example, the increased thickness will preclude fixing by adhesive. In this situation, special steel fixings will be required.

left French limestone tiles in a small bathroom make a refreshing change from the more ubiquitous ceramic tiling.

below In a stunning open-plan space, travertine marble flooring and pillars separate television area from wooden-floored sitting room.

left **A rustic country hearth constructed out of irregularly shaped blocks of fieldstone makes a bold, monumental focal point in a contemporary living room.**

below **A flagstone hearth and hallway floor contrast with a modern fireplace lined in brick and clad in narrow stone tiles.**

stone

worksurfaces

Stone counters make a pleasing graphic contrast to other interior surfaces. Their intrinsic coolness and smoothness is both tactile and practical: marble, for example, provides exactly the right surface for rolling pastry. In bathrooms, stone vanity tops convey a sense of classic understatement. Elsewhere in the home, solid stone can also be used horizontally to create low plinths or shelves, or even tabletops.

Stone for built-in surfaces such as hearths, fire surrounds, vanity tops and kitchen counters is typically supplied in slab form, in thicknesses that range from 2.5cm (1in) to 5cm (2in). The size of slab varies according to the type of stone, which is an important factor to consider if you intend to extend the stone over a large area and wish to avoid the interruption of joints. Many suppliers will cut stone to specified shapes and sizes if they are provided with a scale drawing.

Choice of stone will depend on use. Porous stones, such as limestone, are not suitable for use as kitchen counters or in situations where there is a risk of scratching. Hard dense stones such as granites and slates are more suitable. Any counter made of stone may be damaged by thermal

below **A slab of granite, polished only on top, creates a rugged worksurface in a country kitchen with whitewashed rubblestone walls.**

above **Beautiful and basic: a reclaimed marble worktop provides a contemporary take on country style in a cottage kitchen.**

below **A slab of Belgian blue stone makes a spare, minimal worktop inset with flush square hobs and square sink cutouts.**

above **Glossy black marble makes a superb worksurface, with inset drainage grooves.**

shock: never place hot pans or dishes directly on top or the stone may crack.

Stone worksurfaces require some form of framework, which must be adequately robust to bear the weight of the material and provide support at close enough intervals. In general, stone slabs are fixed with a proprietary adhesive. Using additional features such as fascias and splashbacks made from matching stone provides a neat finishing touch.

stone

above **The essence of purity: standing on a marble floor, a simple rectangular-shaped marble bath, with a minimally detailed single tap rising directly from the floor, preserves the serene contemplative nature of empty space.**

other uses

Stone is such a monumental material that it is not often considered as a way of adding decorative embellishment or of creating focal points. Yet stone accessories and fittings are increasingly available. These details provide an original twist to the interior, together with a sense of timelessness.

Some of the most evocative stone fittings are stone baths and basins, available

below left **A marble basin poised on a metal bracket reduces washing to its most elemental.**

below centre **An old stone trough, framed with stainless steel, serves as a washbasin.**

below right **A simple marble pedestal sink has a strong sculptural presence.**

in a range of different types of stone, including limestone, granite and marble and in standard or bespoke formats. These simple tub and bowl shapes, seemingly hewn from the rock, polished smooth or honed to a more granular texture, have an elemental simplicity that elevates bathrooms to temples of bathing.

Stone mouldings and decorative borders are also widely available. Such mouldings can be used either as trim or finishing touches for fire surrounds or work-surfaces, as dados, skirting boards or as a way of framing mirrors, mosaics and other surface finishes.

Found stone and stone accessories provide more or less instant ways of pursuing the stone aesthetic. Shallow stone platters or bowls create table-top focal points; heaps of beachstones, smoothed by the sea, make simple floor-level displays. Because of environmental concerns, you should buy stones rather than collect them yourself from the beach.

care and maintenance

Stone is widely regarded as tough and hard, with the result that it is commonly imagined not to require much in the way of maintenance. Nevertheless, sealing will provide an important barrier to the build-up of dirt and grime and will prolong the quality of finish. This is especially important in the case of limestone and sandstone, which are porous and will stain readily unless sealed. Stone represents something of an investment, and adequate care and maintenance is only sensible.

All types of stone, whether used for flooring or cladding, should be sealed prior to grouting to prevent stains that might occur during laying or installation. After grouting, the final surface should also be sealed – up to three times in the case of

porous types of stone such as limestone and sandstone. Most large stone suppliers have their own proprietary sealant. Worksurfaces are often available ready-sealed. All seals should be renewed periodically; consult the manufacturer's guidelines.

Types of stone with a pitted texture, such as certain limestones, particularly travertine, are often supplied 'pre-filled', or with the pits already filled in. In time, some of these fillings may work loose and require replacement.

For stone flooring, routine maintenance involves brushing or vacuuming to pick up loose dirt and dust, together with localized scrubbing with water and a neutral detergent; you may need to clean textured surfaces more frequently than smooth or honed flooring. Avoid mopping stone floors,

as this only serves to deposit a dirty film across the surface. Spills should be tackled straight away with a damp cloth, moistened with water or, in the case of grease or oil spills, with white spirit. Stone cladding requires little more than periodic vacuuming and worksurfaces can generally be maintained simply by wiping over with a damp cloth. Avoid the use of scouring powders and powerful abrasive detergents.

Acids of various descriptions can discolour stone. Tackle any spill of wine, citrus juice, cola or vinegar immediately. Oils and wax polishes should also be avoided as these have a tendency to create stains.

below **Vivid veining on the Carrara marble floor and wall tiles makes an effective contrast to stainless-steel units.**

glass

left **Expanses of glass bring an unbeatable sense of drama to the interior, as well as maximizing light and views. Perhaps the ultimate in theatricality is a glass floor. This bathroom floor, which extends to the hallway, is made of 25mm (1in) laminated glass with a translucent interlayer.**

right **A motorized rooflight slides back to create an open-air dining space. The rooflight is made of double-glazed panels of low-emissivity glass, a type developed to prevent excessive heat loss or gain.**

left **Large walls infilled with glass dramatically light a double-height space in Paris.**

right **A steel-framed glazed panel pivoting at its midpoint seamlessly connects interior and exterior areas.**

Glass is one of the most magical of all materials. Three and a half thousand years ago in the Middle East it was discovered that, with the application of heat, soda, lime and sand formed a hard, transparent material. Ever since, glass-making has undergone a more or less constant process of technological development. Once purely decorative in application, glass is now a thoroughly architectural material, and the futuristic concept of the glass house has become a reality.

In Northern Europe, from the fifteenth century onwards, glass was used more frequently to cover windows and other openings. In the great Gothic cathedrals, soaring stained-glass windows with their tracery of supporting stonework were literally identified with divine light, while Biblical scenes portrayed in coloured glass provided an inspirational and instructive text for illiterate congregations.

The scale and design of early windows reflected the technological development of the material itself. The gridded appearance of the casement window of the fifteenth and sixteenth centuries, for example, is a consequence of the fact that, at this period, glass could only be produced in relatively restricted sizes. These small panes needed to be pieced together in the characteristic lead framework to make a window of any significant size at all.

Glass, of course, has always been valued for its transparency, but it is important to remember that in the early stages of its development glass was not the crystal-clear material with which we are familiar today. The sparkling façades of early manor houses, with their many small panes glinting in the sun, belie the fact that the glass was of such low transparency that it was only just possible to see through it.

By the eighteenth century, glass production had progressed and the material was cheaper, more transparent and could be manufactured in larger sizes. The elegant sash windows that are so notable a feature of eighteenth-century architecture reflect both these advances and the prevailing taste for interiors to be as light and bright as possible.

In nineteenth-century public and commercial buildings, however, glass achieved a new architectural virtuosity. Cheap rolled plate glass was available from the mid-century onwards. Winter gardens, conservatories, the lofty roofs of railway stations and shopping arcades provided a convincing demonstration of the dramatic potential of the material.

Until the Industrial Revolution, the size of windows and other openings was restricted by the fact that structural systems consisted of load-bearing walls – openings could not be extensive or numerous without weakening the building. But as the framed structure developed, in cast iron and later in steel, the architectural potential of glass was dramatically increased. In a framed structure, walls are merely infills, not supporting elements, which raises the tantalizing possibility of walls made entirely of glass.

These structural developments coincided with a marked improvement in the quality of glass itself. In the 1920s new processes enabled plate glass to be produced economically in large sizes and with a crystal-clear transparency. At the same time, early modernists such as Mies van der Rohe and Walter Gropius were quick to recognize how glass could be used to redefine the way in which buildings related to their surroundings. Traditional Japanese houses, with their translucent rice-paper screens forming flexible boundaries and partitions, were an important source of inspiration and reference. Mies's German Pavilion at the International Exhibition in Barcelona (1929) is the first realization of a glass house on a domestic scale. Walls made entirely of glass supported by a fine steel framework dissolved the boundaries between indoors and out and transformed interior spatial relationships.

Another seminal example is the Maison de Verre (1931) in Paris, designed by Pierre Chareau, which features a soaring double-height wall of glass. This wall forms the façade of the house and is composed of many translucent glass blocks, preserving the privacy of the interior and forming a soft, glowing background to the main living spaces.

Another technological leap came in 1959, with the invention of float glass by the British manufacturer Pilkington. The process produced glass of a uniform thickness, brightness and clarity. Glass had finally come of age as an architectural material. Pre-dating the invention of float glass by a decade, both Mies van der Rohe's Farnsworth House in 1950 and Philip Johnson's Glass House in 1949 had graphically demonstrated the contemporary design possibilities of fully transparent walls.

In the contemporary interior, change has been equally dramatic. Glass has long been used as an infill for interior partitions and doors but in recent years more theatrical uses have come to the fore, in the shape of cutting-edge features such as glass floors and walkways, glass baths and basins. In any application, the sparkle and transparency of the material adds a new dimension and dynamic to the quality of space.

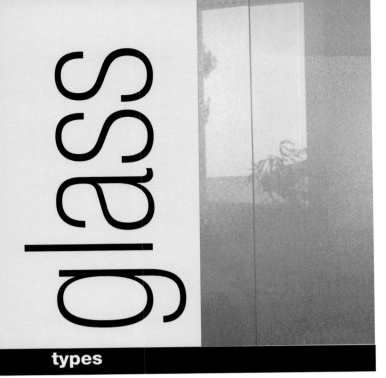

glass

relatively minimally, modern expanses of glass have greater implications for heat loss and gain, safety and security. Consequently, many recent innovations in glass manufacture have been concerned with such practical and environmental issues. In the near future, it is envisaged that glass will become a fully interactive material, a 'dynamic skin' that reacts instantly to changes in heat and light. One type of glass already on the market is designed for large areas where privacy is sometimes an issue. A triple-layered glass 'sandwich', it becomes opaque when an electric current flows through it.

Basic types of manufacture

Float glass During the float-glass process, a continuous ribbon of molten glass approximately 3m (10ft) wide and heated to a thousand degrees Centigrade is poured out of a furnace into a bath of molten tin. The glass floats on the tin, levels out and is gradually cooled until it is hard enough not to be marked by rollers. Then it is

above **Glass makes effective internal partitions, separating areas of activity without blocking light. This textured glass panel in a bathroom provides an element of privacy.**

right **A skylight positioned directly above a glass staircase dramatically emphasizes the sense of lightness and transparency.**

Glass is a much more varied material than might first be supposed. There are, of course, the obvious variations of colour, pattern and opacity but more significant are differences in performance and method of manufacture. Such technical specifications, which are rarely immediately apparent, have considerable relevance when it comes to the choice of glass for a particular application.

Because glass has been the subject of continual technical development, the terminology can be confusing. Terms such as 'plate' and 'sheet' are in common usage to describe any large expanse of glass, no matter how it has been produced. Properly speaking, 'plate' and 'sheet' actually refer to specific and now largely superseded methods of manufacture. Today, 90 percent of all flat glass produced in the world is made by the float glass process.

The arrival of float glass did not, however, halt the process of refinement, but ushered in a new era of technological development. As the applications of glass have expanded, so have the demands on performance. Unlike previous centuries when glass was used

above **New types of glass include a glass that can be made opaque at the flick of a switch, a property that has been exploited in this panel dividing bedroom from bath.**

Strengthened glass

Because glass is such a brittle material and potentially so damaging when it shatters or breaks, considerable research and development has gone into devising ways of improving its strength and resistance to impact. Strengthened glass is not only safer than standard glass, it is also more secure.

Wired glass Wired glass consists of a fine steel mesh sandwiched between two separate layers of glass. The wire mesh increases the strength of the glass and holds fragments in place after shattering. The result is an exceptionally tough glass product which can be used where there is the need for increased security or fire-resistance. Wired glass is made by the rolling process and may have a surface pattern or be fully transparent.

Toughened glass Also known as tempered glass, toughened glass is an important safety product with widespread applications for internal and external glazing. To make it, glass is heated to 650 degrees Centigrade, then rapidly chilled so that the outer layers of glass solidify before the inner core has fully cooled. As the core cools, it compresses the outer surfaces and thus imparts a high degree of strength, up to five times that of annealed glass. When toughened glass is fractured, it breaks into tiny harmless pieces.

passed through an annealing lehr where further controlled cooling takes place. The eventual result is perfectly flat glass, with a fine 'fire-polished' surface and uniform thickness.

Float glass can be manufactured in a variety of thicknesses to suit different applications and specifications, from less than 2mm (1/16in) to over 2.5cm (1in). Maximum available sizes depend on thickness and the limitations of shipping and handling. For thicknesses up to 1.2cm (1/2in), the maximum size is 31.8m x 60.80m (103ft 3in x 200ft); for thicknesses over 1.2cm (1/2in), the maximum size is smaller. To make standard panes, the extreme edges of the molten-glass ribbon are scored with tungsten-carbide cutting wheels while the ribbon is still moving and the panes are snapped off automatically.

Rolled glass Aside from float glass, the other basic form of glass manufacture is rolled glass. In this process, glass in a semi-molten state is pressed between rollers to create a ribbon of uniform thickness and a specific surface pattern. Rolling is used to make wired glass and patterned glass.

Types of glass widely available include: standard window glass (1), etched glass (2) and wired glass (3). Wired glass is a popular choice for glazed door panels, or where there is a need for increased security.

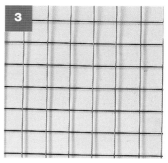

If toughened glass is worked in any fashion after the toughening process has been carried out, it will shatter, so it must be made to size. Maximum sizes are also limited by the process. Wired glass cannot be toughened.

Laminated glass Laminated glass was first developed as a safety material for car windows. It consists of a thin transparent layer of plastic sandwiched between two sheets of glass, the whole bonded together by heating under pressure. The particular safety advantage of this type of glass is that the inner layer serves to hold the fragments of glass in place after impact or breakage. It is generally considered safer than toughened glass and is more expensive.

Different thicknesses, types of glass and types of inner layer can be combined to create a wide range of products with different practical and visual properties. Multiple layers of toughened and laminated glass produce bullet-proof glass.

Glass and energy

It has long been appreciated that expanses of glass can have a dramatic impact on the climate indoors, creating extreme variations in temperature. On warm, bright days, heat can rapidly build up to an unacceptable degree; on dull, cool days, heat loss can be equally abrupt and uncomfortable. Plant houses and conservatories make obvious practical use of this 'greenhouse effect'; in other circumstances, it is far less welcome.

If glass is not modified in any way, a temperate internal environment can only be maintained by extra heating in winter and air conditioning in summer, which in turn has a deleterious impact on energy consumption. At the same time, a certain degree of passive heat gain from glazing can help to reduce energy consumption overall. Set against these considerations is the need to maintain light levels and transparency.

The precise relationship between glass and solar energy is extremely technical and complex. But it is enough to understand that there are various ways in which glass can be treated or modified to prevent extreme interior conditions. These include tinting, multiple glazing and specialist coatings.

Tinted glass is produced by adding small amounts of metal oxides, such as iron, cobalt and selenium, to the molten mix. Depending on the precise combination of oxides, different colours are produced, typically bronze, grey, green and blue. Tinting increases the amount of heat absorbed by the glass, so that less penetrates through to the interior. But at the same time, less light is also admitted. Reflective glass, developed in the mid-1960s, has a similar effect.

Glazed units have a particular role in reducing heat loss in the interior. These incorporate two or more panes of glass separated by a spacer so that there is a hermetically sealed air-filled gap between the panes. Double-glazed units are standard; high-specification triple-glazed units are also available, as well as those which incorporate adjustable blinds within the layers of glazing.

Low-emissivity (Low-E) glass A recent innovation in glass technology is the development of Low-E coatings which allow maximum daylight into the room but retain the heat at night, acting as a form of thermal insulation. This type of glass is particularly practical for glazed extensions, glazed roofs and other applications where heat loss might be unacceptably high.

left **Full-height metal-framed glass doors provide an elegant connection to the garden.**

Decorative glass

The sparkling appearance of glass can be further enhanced by a wide range of decorative effects involving colour and pattern. In many cases, such treatments are not merely aesthetically pleasing but also serve to increase privacy in situations where full transparency would not be welcome.

Textured glass Glass with a relief pattern is produced either by casting or by impressing a repetitive design onto the semi-molten surface with a roller. Commonly known as obscured glass, such designs have the effect of distorting views without radically decreasing the amount of light and have tended to be used in situations where privacy is desirable – in glazed door panels or bathroom windows, for example. Typical patterns include ridged, pebbled, stippled and rippled surfaces.

above **Original stained glass, such as these door panels dating from 1900–1910, adds decorative and architectural interest.**

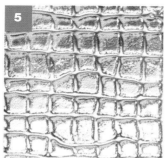

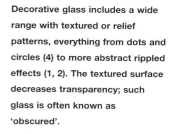

Decorative glass includes a wide range with textured or relief patterns, everything from dots and circles (4) to more abstract rippled effects (1, 2). The textured surface decreases transparency; such glass is often known as 'obscured'.

above and above right **Sandblasting is a versatile technique which can be used to create a range of effects, from deeply carved to surface texture.**

Coloured glass From traditional stained glass to coloured laminate glass, which may be either opaque or translucent, coloured glass brings an extra dimension to the interior. Bespoke designs can be created by glass artists to order and a wide range of traditional or period designs are also available for feature windows or door lights. Architectural salvage yards are a good source.

Etched and sandblasted glass Also known as 'frosted glass', glass which has been surface-treated by sandblasting or acid-etching has a soft, uniform and matt appearance that obscures views and gently

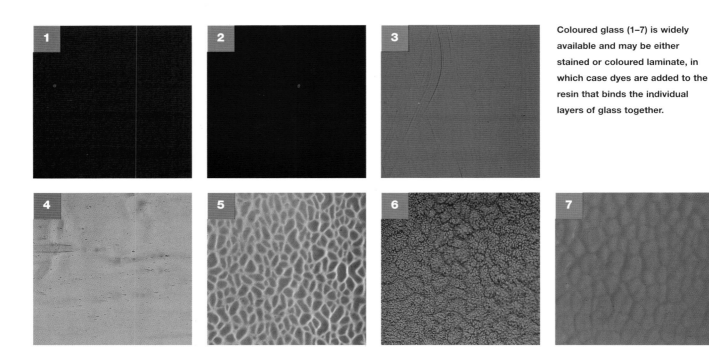

Coloured glass (1–7) is widely available and may be either stained or coloured laminate, in which case dyes are added to the resin that binds the individual layers of glass together.

diffuses light. Again, special designs can be commissioned to order, from simple masked shapes such as circles and stars to more elaborate detail.

Printed glass Another way of decorating glass is by screenprinting. At the simplest level, repeating patterns of dots, lines or hatching serve to create an alternative version of obscured glass without the obvious surface texture; there are also full-blown glass pictures.

Glass blocks

Long before glass assumed its architectural role in modern design, glass blocks represented a way of combining the translucent qualities of the material with structural possibilities. Glass blocks can be used as a stronger, more secure and more obscuring infill for window openings, or as an interior feature to create separate areas without the loss of valuable light. Unlike many standard types of glazing, glass blocks have sound- and heat-insulation qualities. A variety of finishes is available, including clear, frosted, satin, reeded and rippled, depending on the level of transparency required. Glass blocks also come in a range of colours, with intense blues, turquoises and aquamarines being among the most effective.

Mirror

Mirror glass has a long history of development, with the finest early examples being produced in Venice. Such mirrors were made of silvered blown glass, a process that naturally limited the size. The only way to create a more extensive mirrored surface was to piece individual panes together, a method used to create the famous Hall of Mirrors at Versailles. It was not until the late seventeenth century, in France, that large sheets of glass were first produced by casting. Mirrors large and tall enough to reflect the entire figure were a considerable novelty.

Personal vanities aside, the ability of mirror to multiply views and reflect light has long been prized in interior decoration, especially in northern climates where light levels are naturally low. As soon as mirror-making improved, mirrored surfaces began to appear everywhere – on door panels, on ceilings, above chimneypieces – adding a glittering dimension to finely detailed rooms.

Today, mirror is made by silvering glass, which involves chemically coating clear glass with a layer of silver covered with a protective layer of copper and subsequently finished with a backing

above **Textured glass blocks are used to create a curved wall enclosing a shower. Professional installation is recommended.**

of paint. Size and scale is no longer a technical problem, and mirror is available in a range of sizes from large uninterrupted expanses, suitable for covering a wall, right down to tiny adhesive-backed mirror tile and mirror mosaic.

Glass blocks (1–3) come in a range of colours and a variety of finishes, from clear through frosted to rippled.

applications

glass

left **An extensive glass shelf lit from underneath creates a gentle, diffused source of ambient light.**

The use of glass in the interior is indivisible from that essential element, natural light. The transparency of glass allows our homes to be saturated in daylight – the ultimate feel-good factor; but it also has a 'look, no hands' quality of visual lightness and lack of substance that gives structures a certain ambiguous, floating quality. Glass, of course, is not light in weight and modern varieties approach the strength of other building materials. But in contemporary designs where flexibility and clarity are prized, glass fulfils an important role in creating divisions between indoors and out and

right **Minimal framing and support mean that contemporary glazed walls or extensions can achieve almost total transparency, dissolving the boundary between indoors and out.**

between individual interior spaces that are as minimal and discreet as possible.

The technological advances in the material mean that it is suitable for a wider range of applications than ever before – a house entirely made of glass, once a futurist's dream, is to all intents and purposes now perfectly achievable. It is, however, possible to have too much of a good thing. Extensive glazed surfaces can have the effect of setting the teeth on edge – and it is not to

everyone's taste to live in an environment that is relentlessly revealing and exposing. In combination with more domestic, solid materials such as wood, or in conjunction with sleek contemporary finishes such as metal, the use of glass need not entail sacrificing a sense of comfort, enclosure or security. Special care should also be taken in situations where the visual ambiguity of glazed partitions or doorways could present a hazard, particularly for young children.

below left **A variation on the theme of French windows has glazed metal framed doors set in a glass surround to maximize light and views.**

below **Windows subdivided by the gridded pattern of glazing bars are often inherently more interesting than picture windows comprising uninterrupted planes of glass. The glass vanity top adds to the feeling of lightness and transparency.**

applications

glass

down through the levels and creating a feeling of expansiveness. This strategy is particularly invaluable in terraced houses where windows are generally restricted to front and back and the quality of light may lack a certain dynamism.

above **A curved glass screen encloses a metal stairway to provide a transparent means of fire-proofing. The glass doors are framed in lacquered metal.**

below **Coloured glass tubes containing household liquids such as shampoo and foam bath make an eye-catching, artist-designed focal point at a window.**

external openings

The design of windows and the technical development of glass has, to a great extent, gone hand in hand – from the fifteenth- and sixteenth-century leaded casement windows, to the eighteenth- and nineteenth-century sash and the contemporary metal-framed picture window. Sensitivity to the style and period of your house is important when it comes to choice of external glazing. There is no surer way of undermining architectural character than by replacing original windows with modern double-glazed units. For traditional homes, period door lights with painted or stained glass inserts provide a decorative flourish at the entranceway; salvage yards and antique dealers are good sources of original examples reclaimed from old houses and buildings. Panes of coloured glass can also make an effective substitution in hall windows, doors and as fanlights. Frosted or etched panes are similarly in keeping with traditional design.

In contemporary settings and in the design of modern extensions and conservatories, the scope in terms of scale and detailing is far greater. Full- or part-glazed extensions at ground level help to bring natural light into existing parts of the house and reinforce the connection with the outside. In a similar way, replacing a door with a double doorway, French windows or even an entire wall of glass can transform the quality of internal spaces. It can be argued, however, that an entire wall of glass can have a certain static quality, reducing a view to a featureless backdrop. Even in modern contexts, the rhythm of supporting frameworks that subdivide glass into individual panels can be more animating than the blank stare of an uninterrupted plane.

If you prefer a greater degree of enclosure and privacy, light levels can still be maintained by glazing the roof of the extension. Special care should be taken to ensure that roof glazing is properly installed so that it is watertight. This may entail the use of a structural silicone sealant which bonds the glass into its framework and cures to form a durable weatherproof seal. Alternatively, some companies produce roofing systems that are ready made in standard units to be assembled in situ.

Top-lighting in general has a dramatic effect on the sense of space. Installing a rooflight or skylight at the head of a staircase is a good way of spilling light

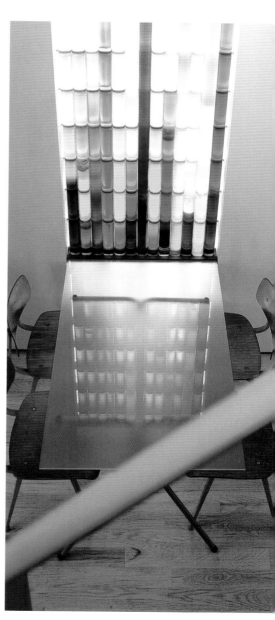

flooring

Glass flooring is the closest we ever get to walking on air. The theatricality of the experience, coupled with the potential for evocative light effects, makes glass flooring one of the most impressive applications to be found.

Glass is far from a mainstream flooring choice and is not suitable for extensive areas. But as a mezzanine walkway, or in the form of cantilevered or spiral stairs, glass flooring allows light and views to remain uninterrupted from level to level. A similar effect can be achieved by removing a portion of flooring around the perimeter of an upstairs room and infilling with glass, thus creating a floor-level window that allows light through to spaces below. Another floor-level effect is to construct display boxes sunk flush with the floor and topped with glass strong enough to walk on. One such example, located in a bathroom, was filled with seashells; in another version of the same idea, ostrich eggs were used to add to the sense of fragility.

Careful specification, engineering and installation are required. The type of glass suitable for flooring is thick annealed float

glass

glass. Sandblasted friction bars will mitigate against extreme slipperiness. In domestic applications the appropriate specification from the point of view of strength comprises a top layer 2cm (¾in) thick laminated to a 1cm (⅜in) thick base. Because this type of glass is heavy and awkward to manipulate, it is often best to use metre-square (3ft 3in-square) panels. The panels should be slotted into a wooden or metal framework that supports all four sides, with an infill of neoprene rubber cushioning.

above **A steel-framed glass staircase and walkway provide uninterrupted views from level to level.**

opposite, above **Textured panels of etched dots – known as friction bars – protect from slipping on a dramatic stairway.**

opposite **Ribbed glass panels set in a wooden floor and frosted glass dividers and cupboard fronts give a sense of light.**

below **Glass flooring requires careful specification and engineering so can be expensive. The bonus is unbeatable drama.**

glass

right **This shower screen demonstrates how good glass blocks look when used wholeheartedly to make a generous infill. The walls are of polished plaster.**

below **Translucent glass panels framed in metal enclose a kitchen area within an open-plan space. The panels can be slid back and forth as required.**

internal partitions

Glass is an ideal material for constructing internal partitions and divisions. Its transparency provides a degree of separation between different activities or zones of the interior without compromising either the views through a space or the sense of expansiveness. Internal glazing also allows light to spill through from area to area, which is a particular advantage in buildings that receive little in the way of direct natural light.

Glazed partitions can take two forms: structural divisions, and sliding or fixed non-structural panels. In the former case, the preferred material is glass blocks or bricks which are strong in compression and function essentially like any other building block. Although glass bricks have become something of a cliché in contemporary interiors, they are an effective means of screening, particularly in situations where total transparency would be a drawback, for example, when enclosing a bathroom or shower. Glass bricks look best when they are used in a generous wholehearted fashion, not as meagre infills.

Because of the weight of the material, it is advisable to consult a surveyor to determine whether the sub-floor will bear the additional load imposed by the construction. Glass-brick divisions are best constructed by professionals with experience in the use of the material; specialist mortars will also be required.

below **A sheet of sandblasted glass provides a semi-transparent screen for a staircase made of Australian jarrah wood.**

above **Translucent glass panels framed in metal provide screening for clothes storage.**

Glass blocks can also be used to make non-structural partitions and in this instance construction is very much simpler and quicker. Some suppliers manufacture frame systems which obviate the need for mortar fixing: the framework must be fixed on at least three sides and then the glass blocks are pushed into place and retained with rubber gaskets.

Sliding or pivoting panels of glass, glass screens framed in timber or metal, glazed internal doorways, windows, lights and panels all serve to open out interior spaces and add flexibility. Careful specification, with regard both to type of glass and method of framing, is essential.

glass

fittings and fixtures

Glass has many small-scale applications in the home which are no less effective for being unmomentous. The lightness of glass shelving focuses attention on what is being displayed and provides an unbeatable way of emphasizing the luminous transparency of glassware and decorative glass objects, particularly when combined with sensitive accent lighting. In a similar way, glass-fronted kitchen units and bathroom cabinets are far less dominating than those with solid doors, an effect which is particularly welcome where space is at a premium. Many outlets supply ready-made glass shelving, complete with fixings, for easy assembly and installation. Wipe-clean glass splashbacks provide an easy-maintenance solution in kitchens and bathrooms.

Many types of light fitting exploit the sparkle and diffusion of glass. Frosted globes provide good sources of all-round illumination; shades featuring coloured glass inserts have a jewelled intensity. Glass chandeliers and sconces, with their facetted

above **Bathing at its most elemental – in a moulded glass tub. Glass fittings and furniture have a 'look no hands' quality that lends drama to an interior.**

below **Another essay in minimalism, this glass tank tub makes use of structural sealant rather than obvious framing or supports.**

crystal drops, add an unbeatable sense of theatricality and glitter to the surroundings.

Glass has been used increasingly in the design of contemporary bathroom fittings, a notable example being handbasins in the form of clear, coloured or frosted-glass bowls. But perhaps the ultimate in visual lightness are bathtubs completely made of glass. Glass has been used safely for many years in aquaria and swimming pools to make observation panels; in the case of bathtubs, the minimal detailing and lack of supporting frames is achieved with structural sealant.

right **An expanse of mirror increases the sense of space and multiplies the effect of natural light. Here a mirrored wall at right angles to a large window serves to visually broaden a bathroom.**

below **This stainless-steel kitchen has a glass work surface and shelves of 'nibbled' glass for the ultimate clean-lined look.**

below right **A mirrored end wall opens out a small bathroom. The floor tiles are of glass mosaic.**

safety and security

People in glass houses should . . . be careful. When ordinary glass breaks, it fractures into razor-sharp splinters that can cause serious and, in certain cases, life-threatening injury. It is not merely the brittleness of glass and its propensity to shatter that consititutes the hazard, but also the fact that transparency renders a glazed barrier less immediately visible. Particular danger zones have been identified by safety studies. These include doors – such as French windows – glazed panels around doors, glazing at low level and any area where the floor may become wet and increase the risk of slipping and colliding with a glazed partition or panel.

The strength of glass can be increased to prevent breakage up to a certain degree of impact; beyond this point, it is a question of ensuring that when glass breaks, it does so safely, either by disintegrating into 'dice' or by fracturing in such a way that individual splinters continue to be held together. The safest types of glass are wired, toughened and laminated, with laminated delivering the best all-round safety specification. Glass which is both toughened and laminated delivers optimum strength. These types of glass should always be specified for any high-risk application, particularly in a family home. Alternatively, standard glass can be customized with safety film which serves a similar purpose to lamination by holding shattered glass together following impact.

In most applications, glass will be held within a framework that secures all four edges. But in certain situations, such as shelving, table tops or other semi-fitted horizontal planes, sharp edges and corners may be exposed. Glass edges should always be ground smooth so there is no risk of accidental cuts, and corners should be protected with plastic caps if there are small children in the home.

Glass floors and stairs present the obvious hazard of possible slipperiness. Friction bars sandblasted at intervals across the floor panels will reduce the risk.

Exterior glazing also has implications for security – extensive planes of glass can act rather like a shop window advertising the contents of your home. While a picture window may serve as a deterrent to burglars who would normally wish to avoid the noise and danger involved in breaking an expanse of glass, glazed panels in doors and smaller windows are more vulnerable to attack. Strengthened glass is a good idea in such situations; alarm glass is also available which incorporates electro-conducting circuits that can be wired to an alarm system. External or interior shutters and metal grilles may well be advisable for glazed areas at ground-floor level.

care and maintenance

Despite its rather fragile image, glass is surprisingly durable – there are still intact examples of glass which are eight or nine hundred years old. Cleaning is a different issue. Glass is far from maintenance-free and demands a fairly high degree of vigilance to stay looking pristine and sparkling. A fairly unforgiving surface when it comes to fingerprints and other greasy marks, glass inevitably reveals every single smudge and streak the instant it is made. Some research has gone into the development of non-stick coatings – with the aim of reducing maintenance, particularly for the windows of high-rise buildings – but in most domestic situations the solution remains a good astringent cleaning product, a supply of lint-free clean cloths and plenty of elbow grease.

left **Glass makes an inconspicuous and practical splashback, but can be demanding in terms of maintenance.**

opposite **Frosted, etched or sandblasted glass give privacy while not blocking out light. Here a clear square 'window' in a semi-opaque shower screen provides a glimpse of a view.**

metal

left **Utilitarian and basic or
sleek and sophisticated, metal
is a material increasingly seen
in domestic applications.
This partition wall made of
corrugated metal is simple
and unpretentious.**

right **A spiral staircase in
stainless steel leads to a landing
floored in metal landscape
grating – an effective borrowing
from a non-domestic context.**

above **A roof made of lightweight industrial tin soars over a vaulted metal-framed space infilled with glass.**

The metal aesthetic is sharp and defiantly hard-edged. Gleaming steel and glass high-rise blocks define the modern cityscape all over the world. Widespread use in the aeronautical industry, combined with a more rough-and-ready role in temporary commercial structures and as a common factory finish, means that materials such as aluminium and galvanized steel also bring with them a certain quality of basic utility. At the same time, metal surfaces and finishes can impart a look of sleek efficiency, an association derived equally from the research lab, clad in gleaming stainless steel, and the professional kitchen.

For early modernists, metal was truly a wonder material. In a rousing polemic, 'Wood or Metal?', published in *The Studio* in 1929, Charlotte Perriand, who collaborated with Le Corbusier in the creation of his most famous furniture designs, wrote: 'The EIFFEL TOWER could never have been made of Wood. Metal is superior to wood; reasons? The power of resistance in metal itself; Because it allows of mass production in the factory (lessens amount of labour

above **Curved walls are lined in custom-designed metal mesh screens, the central screen framing a sleek contemporary fireplace.**

required); Because by means of the different methods of manufacture it opens out new vistas; new opportunities of design; Because the protective coatings against toxic agencies not only lower the cost of upkeep, but have considerable AESTHETIC value. METAL plays the same part in furniture as cement has done in architecture. IT IS A REVOLUTION.'

Iron and its derivative steel are the most common metals used in construction. As building materials, they are very strong, which means they can be used minimally, but they are also comparatively expensive and prone to corrosion, which often necessitates some form of protection from the elements. Their use has therefore corresponded to the development of the framed structure.

This development was inaugurated by Abraham Darby of Coalbrookdale in Shropshire, England. He devised a method of smelting iron with coke in the second half of the eighteenth century. This process increased the quality of

right **Shiny corrugated aluminium provides an original splashback in an all-metal kitchen.**

the basic material, led to a corresponding fall in prices and paved the way for a dramatic expansion of the market. The first significant cast-iron structure anywhere in the world was Iron Bridge (1779) at Coalbrookdale, which spanned 30 metres (100ft) across the River Severn and was designed by Abraham Darby's son. There were no precedents for such construction; the need for precise calculation of the profiles and strength of individual elements marked the beginning of the collaboration between engineer and architect in the realization of buildings and other structures, a partnership that underpins contemporary design.

As the Industrial Revolution got underway, cast iron found a role in the construction of early factories. In subsequent decades, more dramatic developments displayed the potential of material to create light, airy enclosures. Buildings such as Paxton's Crystal Palace in London (1851) with its iron-framed roof infilled with glass, Decimus Burton's Palm House at Kew in London (1848) with its roof composed of glass over cast-iron ribs, and Labrouste's Bibliothèque Sainte Geneviève in Paris (1843–50), where delicate cast-iron columns supported a soaring vaulted roof are striking examples. More functionally, cast iron was employed in the construction of many great nineteenth-century railway terminals to create the vast roof spans necessary for train halls. The Gare St Lazare in Paris (1851–2), memorably depicted in a series of oil paintings by Claude Monet, featured cast-iron and wrought-iron roof trusses.

But the story of iron and steel is really the story of the first all-American building type: the high-rise. The next great advance in the use of iron came in late-nineteenth-century Chicago, following the great fire of 1871 that devastated the entire city centre. During the fire, exposed cast-iron beams and columns had melted but those encased in masonry or concrete had not. The lesson was learnt and effective fireproofing spurred the development of the multistoreyed office building and paved the way for the emergence of the first skyscrapers. By the end of the nineteenth and the beginning of the twentieth centuries, tall buildings were being constructed in Chicago and New York where all the loads were carried by skeleton metal frameworks safely hidden behind masonry cladding.

Steel, a relative newcomer in the field of materials, was developed in response to the need for a metal with greater structural strength. Henry Bessemer, the father of the modern steel industry, experimented with different steel-making processes in the latter part of the nineteenth century and eventually set up his own steel works in Sheffield. In the

United States, notable early uses of steel were in the Home Insurance Building in Chicago in 1885 and the framework which Eiffel designed for the Statue of Liberty in 1883.

It was the Modern Movement, with its espousal of the new industrial materials of steel and concrete and the arrival of the skyscraper, that marked steel as the definitive structural material of the twentieth century. The early high-rise office buildings in Chicago comprised bolted steel sections clad in brick or stone; in time these gave way to entire steel frameworks with extensive use of glass on the outer walls. Within decades, steel-frame buildings were towering over the streets of Chicago and Manhattan: the 60-storey Woolworth Building in New York was completed in 1913; the Art Deco extravaganza, the 77-storey Chrysler Building was finished in 1929; a year later, the definitive skyscraper and, for 40 years the world's tallest building, the Empire State, topped out at 102 storeys.

Although steel frameworks (and advances in lift technology) made such great heights attainable, early skyscrapers did not necessarily express a steel aesthetic. While many early modernists had a preference for concealing the steel framework, others such as Walter Gropius and Mies van der Rohe delighted in revealing it. Mies's German Pavilion at the International Exhibition in Barcelona in 1929 featured chromium-plated steel columns. His subsequent work in the United States and the work of his disciples took this approach even further. Mies's campus for the Illinois Institute of Technology, as well as Farnsworth House, 1951 and Lake Shore Drive, 1951 signalled the arrival of steel as a major architectural material.

A very different type of metal aesthetic can be seen in the hugely influential Eames House, California, built in 1949 by Charles and Ray Eames. This brightly coloured steel-frame house was assembled like a kit of parts, with all the elements pre-fabricated and sourced from catalogues. The same friendly and domestic use of metal reappeared several decades later in the brief fad for high-tech, a style largely based on creative salvage. In this context, salvage can be seen to include not only the recyling of second-hand components but also the lateral application of commercial and industrial fittings and fixtures to a domestic setting. Although high-tech did not last long as a full-blown style, in some sense it has never really gone away, maturing into a more sophisticated approach to sourcing ideas and inspiration for the home. To some extent, high-tech also informs those 'inside-out' structures such as Richard Rogers' Lloyds Building in London and Rogers' and Piano's Pompidou Centre in Paris, where not merely the steel framework but also the servicing are defiantly exposed to view.

The use of iron and more particularly of steel has made possible entire new architectural forms. While urban skylines continue to be dominated by towers of glass and steel, steel frameworks have also redefined domestic space. Without the need for solid load-bearing walls and internal supports, houses can be light, airy and open, with fully glazed walls and roofs providing ultimate transparency, and with internal layouts free from any conventional divisions. In recent decades, there has also been an increased willingness to accept metal as a final finish indoors. Metal may be highly processed, but it has almost acquired the status of a natural material. Professional and functional, pristine and sophisticated, metal adds a contemporary edge to the material mix.

metal

types

above **Highly reflective, steel makes a sleek finish for high-tech kitchen units.**

Iron

Iron is found all over the world, although the largest deposits are in North and South America. It is made from iron ore, smelted in a blast furnace. The process involves continually blasting hot air into a mixture of iron ore, coke and limestone until a temperature of 1300 degrees Centigrade is reached. The result is pig iron. Pig iron contains up to 10 percent other elements, up to 4 percent of which may be carbon.

Cast iron is extremely strong in compression, which means that it can support great weights, but it is very brittle. It can be shaped when molten by pouring into moulds – simple oil-bound sand moulds were used for centuries to make firebacks and other fittings. It is more resistant to corrosion than wrought iron.

Wrought iron is very malleable and has high tensile strength, which means that it can withstand pulling and twisting. It contains less carbon than cast iron and is made by adding iron oxide to molten pig iron until the iron becomes purer and less fluid. When it is semi-molten, wrought iron can be worked by hammering and stretching; pieces can also be melted together – a process familiar from the traditional blacksmith's forge. Before the eighteenth century, almost all iron artefacts, aside from weaponry and other cast items, were hand-wrought at the forge: horseshoes, latches, handles, locks and

below **Metal lends itself to decorative effects as in the case of these unusual green-painted banisters on a spiral staircase.**

Metals, which ultimately derive from ores mined from the earth, are conventionally divided into two groups: noble metals and base metals. Noble metals – such as gold, silver, copper and mercury – are found in a pure state in the earth's crust and are lustrous, opaque and cold to the touch. Base metals – such as iron, lead and aluminium – are more liable to react with the atmosphere once they have been extracted from their ore.

Despite their sleek, impermeable appearance, most of the metals that are used in building or as interior finishes have a natural tendency to rust or corrode. In fact, metals are far more vulnerable in this respect than almost any other group of materials. To counter this inherent propensity to decay, metals are either used in the form of stable alloys (for example, stainless steel) or given a protective coating or finish.

All metals are extremely good conductors of both heat and electricity. Most metals warm up very quickly and lose heat with equal rapidity.

above **Steel is ideal for simple balustrading on a modern staircase.**

Steel

Steel is 98–99 percent iron and is produced by refining pig iron to remove excess carbon and other impurities. Other alloying elements may be added, according to the type of performance required. There are literally hundreds of different types of steel alloys, each with its own unique properties.

Steel is considerably stronger than iron but is very prone to corrosion. It also has the quality of pliability, whereas iron is rigid. Although large-scale production of steel dates only from the mid-nineteenth century, it was made in ancient times in very small quantities by heating cast iron to reduce the carbon content. It was used to make blades and tools. Bessemer's method, which launched the steel industry, involved blowing air through a converter over pig iron, which caused the carbon in the pig iron to combine with the oxygen in the air.

Today, steel is produced by one of two principal methods. In the converter process, unwanted elements in the pig iron are removed by oxidation. In the electro-steel process, scrap iron and steel are melted down in an electric furnace, tapped into ladles and then refined further. Molten steel is then formed into ingots which are further processed, levelled, cut, and finally rolled into various shapes and profiles, from plates and sheets and structural sections to bars and tubes.

hinges, railings and balustrades. After industrialization, most iron-mongery was cast. The use of wrought iron today is limited to decorative purposes.

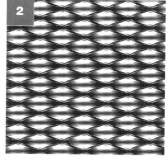

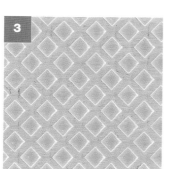

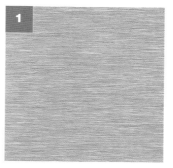

Steel is available in a range of coatings and finishes. Brushed stainless steel (1) has a matt look; rigidized stainless steel (2) offers increased strength. Other relief patterns include gridded (3) and ridged (4).

above **Steel-clad wall units are crisply detailed.**

steel, which may contain up to 20 percent chromium and nickel, is a good example of an alloy steel. It is expensive but is almost entirely maintenance-free.

Various types of coatings and finishes, including paint, lacquer, enamel and acrylic, can be applied to steel to improve its resistance to atmospheric decay, to provide fireproofing, or simply for decorative effect. Many of these finishes require renewal. Galvanizing is the term for coating steel with a protective layer of zinc. More expensively, steel can also be coated in tin or aluminium. Weathering steel, often known by its tradename Cor-ten, is steel which is designed to weather. It has a coating of iron, carbon, copper and phosphorus which forms a protective layer of rust over the surface.

There are a variety of methods of fixing individual steel members, which principally include welding, bolting and riveting. Riveting is not much used any more. Welding is the most economical way of making strong joints but generally needs to be carried out at the factory. Bolting, which can be done on site, is quicker and easier but the necessary holes can weaken the material.

Aluminium

The third most common element in the earth's crust, aluminium is a silvery metal which is highly resistant to corrosion. It is lightweight –

Steel varies in performance according to the presence of other metals. For example, the addition of manganese makes steel more resistant to impact, while tungsten enables steel to withstand high temperatures. Non-alloy steel, or carbon steel, is pure steel and is a common construction material. Low-alloy steel is somewhat harder and more resistant to corrosion, due to the presence of small amounts of chromium, nickel, manganese and copper. Stainless

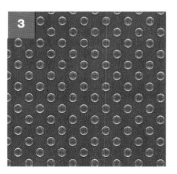

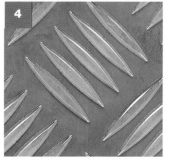

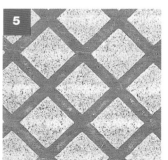

Aluminium's great advantages are its resistance to rusting and the fact that it is very lightweight. Textures include: brushed (1), relief dots in various sizes (2, 3), five-bar (4) and chequered (5).

above **Stairs faced with copper and illuminated with fairy lights beneath each step make a very unusual feature.**

up to three times lighter than steel – which has given it a particular application in the manufacture of aircraft components, and is also very cheap. Aluminium is naturally rather weak but the development of heat-tempered aluminium alloys at the end of the 1930s resulted in materials which were as strong, hard and resilient as steel.

When exposed, the surface of aluminium forms a strong oxide film that resists corrosion but the film can be further thickened by anodizing. The resulting coating is porous and can therefore be dyed to give a decorative effect.

Copper is a warm-toned metal often used to make fireplace hoods and other hearthside features. However, it tarnishes and requires cleaning. It can be polished to a smooth finish (1) or relief-patinated (2, 3).

Zinc

Zinc, like aluminium, is naturally resistant to corrosion and is often used as a plating for steel or iron (the process known as galvanizing). Another type of zinc coating is applied by sherardizing, whereby powdered zinc is fused onto hot metal in a rotating drum. Zinc alloyed with copper makes brass, which is yellowish, stronger than copper and less prone to corrosion. In sheet form, zinc is soft, pliable and prone to scratching.

Copper

Copper has been known since ancient times; its name derives from Cyprus which was the main source of the metal at the time of the Romans. It was in common use for many centuries as a roofing material in northern and eastern Europe. The only brown metal, copper is fairly resistant to corrosion and is a good conductor of electricity. Alloyed with zinc, copper makes brass; alloyed with tin, the result is bronze, which is hard and resistant to corrosion.

Tin

Tin is a white metal, mined since ancient times, and is most commonly used today as a plating for other metals because of its resistance to corrosion. Like aluminium, tin forms an oxide coat which protects the surface from further decay. It is easily worked and not particularly strong.

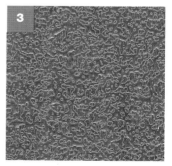

metal

Most homes, even the most traditionally decorated, include a surprising range of metal details: taps and handles, fire irons, hinges and knockers – features that are generally marketed under the umbrella term 'ironmongery' even though they may be made of stainless steel, chrome or brass. Then there are the more prosaic metal features, such as sinks, radiators, lampshades and appliances that barely register as a material use at all. For a thorough-going metal aesthetic, a more expressive use of the material is required – surfaces such as metal splashbacks, countertops or even flooring. Polished metal adds a bright, shiny note that reflects light; matt, brushed surfaces have a soft burnished quality. Enamelled and coated metal finishes come in a range of brilliant glossy colours.

But a little metal goes a long way. A metal-clad interior can bear more than a passing resemblance to a prison cell and it will be relentlessly hard and noisy to boot. Industrial or commercial borrowings are a

above **Stainless steel, with its connotations of hygiene and efficiency, is a popular and practical choice for kitchen surfaces and finishes. Simple steel panels are available which can be applied over existing door fronts for an instant update.**

fruitful source of the metal aesthetic, but you will need to exercise a little restraint or the obvious associations with garages, factory floors and laboratories will be hard to ignore.

frameworks

Metal's great strength means that it can be used to create structures with only a minimal use of the material. It also has a considerable role to play as a supporting framework for glass. These essentially architectural uses can nevertheless have a bearing on interior design, particularly when it comes to creating extensions and new window openings.

Metal and glass have been natural companions for centuries. Fifteenth- and sixteenth-century windows consisted of small panes framed in soft, malleable lead; eighteenth- and early nineteenth-century fanlights often had wrought- or cast-iron glazing bars; while the later nineteenth-century conservatory was a confection of fancy white-painted ironwork infilled with glass.

applications

metal

In the contemporary idiom, structures of steel and glass maximize light and views, dissolving the boundary with outdoor areas. Although the insertion of metal-framed windows into a traditional house front is an architectural solecism of the first order, an abrupt clash of material and style can be highly effective when it comes to creating a rear or rooftop extension.

Metal is also in widespread use to

above **Old scaffolding poles make a rough and ready framework for kitchen fittings.**

above right **Perforated steel panels add textural interest to a staircase.**

right **The kitchen as laboratory, using stainless steel and aluminium.**

create internal mezzanines or platform areas in double-height spaces. At its most rudimentary, a kit-of-parts approach can be adopted, with scaffolding poles jointed together with kee-clamps.

flooring

Not even the most determined modernist would advocate extensive use of metal flooring but in the right situation, both practically and aesthetically, it can provide a very welcome shock of the new. Metal's most common flooring application is in stairways, mezzanine walkways and other transitional areas, where it provides an evocative contrast of texture and appearance to the main flooring surfaces. Then, too, there is the association with

below **An industrial metal ladder provides access to upper levels in a converted water tower. Metal treadplate wrapped around the edge of the raised floor provides visual definition.**

metal

shipboard companionways and overhead gantries, which adds another dimension to the experience of moving from place to place or level to level. Gridded panels or strong metal mesh are particularly effective as semi-transparent floors on upper levels in double-height spaces, their apparent lightness offering minimal disruption of internal views.

Sheet or metal tile can also be used as a final floor covering. Suitable materials include aluminium or galvanized steel; aluminium is the better option if there is a question mark about loading, since it is three times lighter. Industrial-style metal flooring is generally relief-patterned with raised lozenges or dashes (the common term is 'treadplate'); smooth metal sheet or tile must be used with caution due to its extreme slipperiness. The downside of all types of metal floor is that they tend to be cold and noisy.

Lay metal flooring over any level timber or concrete sub-floor. Tiles or sheet can be stuck in place with proprietary adhesive or screwed into position. If the flooring is to be secured by screws, it is a good idea to apply a little adhesive to the underside as well so that the floor does not move or rattle underfoot.

Metal is an important component of many contemporary stair designs, either in

above **The reflective surface of a steel floor adds a sharp edge to this interior and picks up the rosy glow of the fire.**

right **In a penthouse apartment, the interior of the roof vault is made of profiled aluminium sheeting with a painted finish.**

wall to make a splashback, or used to cover basic counters and drawer fronts for a fraction of the cost of steel fitted units.

Corrugated steel sheets are usually coated with aluminium or zinc, or both, and may be painted, galvanized, ceramic- or

left **Perforated metal plate used to make a dividing wall contrasts with smooth concrete flooring.**

right **Ripple iron clads bathroom walls – a simple treatment that will age gracefully.**

below **A steel-clad ceiling has high-tech appeal.**

bottom **Electronically operated perforated aluminium blinds make flexible spatial dividers.**

the form of supports and balustrading or, in the case of spiral stairs, to make the entire framework. A number of companies specialise in custom designs.

cladding

The pliability of many metals means that the material naturally lends itself to cladding; the shiny surface adds sparkle and reflectivity. The softest metal, zinc, is simple to apply to countertops or use as a splashback behind wet areas. The scratches and marks it accumulates with use only add to its appeal. Parisian zinc bars are an obvious source of inspiration. For splashbacks or counters, sheets can be stuck in place using proprietary adhesive; for counters, the edges can be folded under and secured by flat-headed tacks.

Stainless steel makes an ideal kitchen surface, imparting a look of professionalism that derives from its widespread use in catering. Individual thin sheets of steel are widely available from retailers cut to standard sizes or in formats that can be pieced together; these can be stuck to the

metal

left **Off-the-peg commercial metal units and industrial shelving have been adopted to make robust kitchen fittings.**

right **An old kitchen table is updated with a covering of tin.**

far right **A wall-mounted 'prison' style stainless-steel lavatory makes a material contrast with exposed brick walls.**

plastic-coated. Widely used as siding or roofing in lightweight prefabricated sheds and buildings, corrugated metal has a rough-and-ready aesthetic which can bring a kind of raw energy to the interior when used in the form of wall panelling or screens. Corrugated and gridded metal ceiling panels have a high-tech aesthetic.

salvage

Inspired by high-tech, a number of architects and designers are currently exploring the possibilities of heavy-duty salvage, reusing and refashioning a range of items such as oil tanks, storage containers and vehicle parts to create pod-like enclosures for contemporary interiors. Such

robust approaches extend the boundaries of using salvage to a more three-dimensional, even sculptural realm.

More accessible are metal products such as gridded racks for hanging tools, workbenches, industrial sinks, school or sports lockers and a host of other items that can readily be sourced from factory outlets or catalogues and adapted for use in the home. A particular favourite metal fitting amongst architects is the stainless-steel lavatory originally designed for use in prisons. Easy to clean and, unsurprisingly, indestructible, it is a clean-lined contemporary classic.

Junk shops specialising in reclaimed office or commercial furniture from the recent past are another good source of salvageable metal. In many cases, as the vogue for the material has increased, such pieces are available with their regulation grey or green paintwork ready stripped. Filing cabinets and desks that would not normally merit a second glance gain a sleek retro appeal when their gleaming metal finish is exposed.

right **In time metal acquires a pleasing patina of use which does not compromise its performance. These metal kitchen panels have a mottled appearance which softens the effect.**

opposite below **A clean-lined contemporary kitchen is clad in brushed stainless steel. Brushed finishes have a soft appearance.**

below **Zinc is a soft, malleable metal much associated with traditional bar counters of French cafés. Here zinc panels have been used to clad sliding doors.**

details

There are many opportunities to introduce metal on the level of detail, and the result can be to make an interior sharper and more contemporary in mood. A host of metal fittings and furnishings are readily available off-the-peg from retail outlets. Metal storage boxes make durable and attractive systems of home organization; slatted aluminium Venetian blinds combine well with modern styles of decor and are widely available in a range of colours as well as metallic finishes. Metal pendant shades, picture frames, wall racks and other incidental items pursue the same theme.

The simpler styles of metal garden furniture, such as folding café chairs and circular tables often make attractive furnishings indoors as well as out. Less anonymously and more expensively, many of the twentieth century's best known architects have designed chairs that feature

applications

metal

an extensive use of metal. The development of lightweight tubing for bicycle frames inspired early Modernists such as Mies van der Rohe and Marcel Breuer to experiment with cantilevered chair forms, while the arrival of heat-tempered aluminium was marked by Hans Coray's classic lightweight chair whose aluminium seat is punched with holes.

left and below **Stainless steel is increasingly used in modern bathroom fittings to create elemental shapes and forms such as this hemispherical basin and circular tub.**

Metal, of course, has long been a material in common use to make firesurrounds, grates, firebacks and fire irons. Old cast-iron fireplaces were often painted black or white to complement the decor of the room; such finishes can be stripped back to reveal a gun-metal finish which has greater contemporary appeal. Modern steel coal- or wood-burning stoves have a certain sculptural quality and come in a range of colours and textures.

Metal is also increasingly seen in contemporary textile design. Very fine metal mesh is used to create gauzy, semi-transparent fabrics that shimmer and glow with subtle shades of iridescent colour.

left **Metal fixtures, such as taps and handles, provide a graphic edge. Stainless steel is corrosion-proof, but requires a little extra maintenance to remain in a gleaming condition.**

the surface with a couple of coats of matt lacquer. Similarly, if painted or lacquered metal surfaces show signs of flaking or blistering, it may be necessary to renew the finish.

Ordinarily, most metal suitable for use in the interior requires little in the way of maintenance. Stainless-steel surfaces, particularly in the kitchen, are fairly revealing of grease splatters and streaks but can be easily restored to a sparkling finish with scouring powder. Brass requires a little more upkeep and elbow grease. Proprietary cleansers and polishes are also available for brass taps and other fittings which tend to dull and discolour with use.

right **The reflective surface of a brushed stainless-steel unit with integral double sinks enhances the effect of the natural light. The potentially harsh effect of the metal is softened by the lush greenery viewed through the kitchen windows.**

care and maintenance

Corrosion is the enemy of all metals, which is why considerable research has gone into the development of coatings and alloys that resist wear and decay. This, however, tends to be a problem most associated with the use of exposed metal outdoors. Steel will not rust indoors under normal dry conditions.

However, reclaimed metal furnishings, such as office desks and filing cabinets that have been stripped of previous layers of paint may not be proof against rusting or watermarks. This can be a particular problem with stripped-metal bathroom cabinets which are exposed to a humid atmosphere. The solution is to sand off rust patches very gently with wire wool and seal

brick & tile

left **Brick and tilework introduce a pleasing sense of rhythm to interior spaces. Ceramic tiling, laid in blocks of four, defined by crisp grouting, makes a good-looking and practical contemporary floor.**

right **This dramatic brick-clad staircase by the twentieth-century Slovenian architect Joze Plecnik is oval in plan, with a lift shaft passing through the central portion.**

Brick comes from the earth, an origin it shares with many types of hard tile. But there is more than a material common denominator. Scaled to fit the hand, brick and tile are as much about format as they are about composition and methods of manufacture. The rhythmic surface patterns created by the use of these materials are both lively and full of domestic character. Even when machine-made and mass-produced, brick and tile always imply a human connection. All products made of terracotta (literally 'fired' or 'cooked' earth) have an appealing simplicity, a basic, robust quality that is equally at home in rustic or contemporary settings. Modern ceramic tiles have a clean-lined simplicity.

Brick has the distinction of being the most ancient of all man-made building materials. The first bricks – little more than clay mixed with straw and baked hard in the sun – were made over six thousand years ago in the Middle East, using a primitive method which is still evident in the mud or adobe huts of Africa, and Central and Southern America. Terracotta tiles, like brick, have similar origins. Until industrialisation resulted in standardisation, both were strictly local products, made wherever there was a ready supply of clay, such as the areas near to river basins or in alluvial plains. Different clay deposits produced variations of colour and texture. Made with the same ingredients, fired in the same

fashion and often by the same craftsmen, early bricks and tiles displayed even greater similarities than they do today. Medieval bricks, for example, were much thinner than modern types and up to the fifteenth century were commonly known as 'waltyles'.

Brick has long been a standard constructional material in areas of Northern Europe, particularly the Netherlands, Germany and Britain. Here it was associated not only with ordinary domestic buildings, such as the sober Dutch merchant houses of Amsterdam, Leiden and Utrecht and the brick-built terraces of many English towns, but also with fine palaces and churches, such as Hampton Court and Kew in England, with their elaborate twisted chimneystacks. English and Dutch settlers in the New World took their brick-making skills with them and a significant number of North American cities and towns founded before the Revolution feature handsome colonial brick houses. One of the finest is Monticello, Thomas Jefferson's mansion in Virginia. Similarly, British brick traditions were exported to Australia, although the material was most commonly used as a veneer over a timber framework to give buildings a look of superiority. Multi-coloured or polychromatic brickwork, associated with the architecture of the Gothic revival in the nineteenth century, was another European stylistic development that spread far and wide. Ornate, multi-coloured public buildings such as railway stations, churches, libraries and town halls built in brick remain a source of civic pride in many cities around the world.

Today, brick is a material rooted in domesticity. It speaks of tradition and convention, rather than the cutting edge. Yet, throughout the twentieth century, leading designers and architects have convincingly demonstrated that brick can assume a more contemporary role. Frank Lloyd Wright was particularly interested in brick construction, as evidenced in the Robie House, Chicago, where courses of thin bricks emphasize the horizontal lines of the façade. Scandinavian

left **A shower area tiled in crisp mosaic looks out over a garden, with its dividing wall made of roughcast concrete blocks – an effective contrast of scale and finish.**

right **An Indonesian chair sets off an old stone kitchen sink now serving as a washbasin in a mosaic-tiled bathroom with an aged terracotta floor.**

designers such as Alvar Aalto at the 1950 Civic Centre in Saynatsalo, Finland, have also used brick to express the ideals of modernism. Exposed brick floors and walls, with their warmth of colour and evocative texture, provide a foil for clean-lined interiors and minimal furnishing, a welcome echo of comfort and domesticity.

The Romans made extensive use of terracotta floor tiles but the technique, like that of brick-making, seems to have lain dormant until the thirteenth century when it was re-introduced to Spain by the Moors. From Spain, tile-making spread to Northern Europe and, later, to Spanish colonies in Central and Southern America. From these diverse strands comes a wealth of tile-making traditions.

The typical format for handmade terracotta floor tiles or 'pammets' was the 25cm (10in) square. After industrialization, uniform products such as the quarry tile superseded handmade terracotta versions and it has only been in the last few decades, with the renewed interest in natural and authentic forms of decoration, that hand-making has been revived and original antique examples increasingly sought after.

While terracotta tiles are chiefly restricted to flooring applications, glazed tiles offer much greater potential and a stupendous variety of colours, styles and designs. Glazed earthenware tiles date from ninth-century Babylon and the technique was in widespread use throughout the Near East and North Africa for many centuries until it spread to Spain in the fifteenth century. Associated with the rise of Islam, glazed tiles were used to create ravishing and lustrous geometric designs on the floors and walls of royal palaces and mosques – many in abstract patterns of stars and crosses in accordance with the Islamic injunction against representational decoration and art in religious buildings.

Another tile tradition that followed the same path of introduction to western Europe was tin-glazed earthenware. This, again, originated in the Middle East, probably as an attempt to duplicate the whiteness of Chinese porcelain. After firing, the tile was coated in a white glaze and decorated with pigments before being fired again to produce a glossy surface. Italian maiolica was a European development of this technique but its best-known incarnation is undoubtedly Delftware, the blue-and-white chinoiserie-inspired designs produced in the Netherlands and exported all

left **Tiling is inherently domestic. This converted school in Amsterdam, with its plain white tiled walls and black-and-white flooring, makes a cheerful and light-filled home.**

over the world from the seventeenth century onwards. Tiling, in the same way as brick, acquired something of a homely domestic quality. Tiled floors and walls were fresh and cheerful and easy to keep clean. In dairies and stillrooms, tiling helped to maintain the cool temperature essential for keeping food fresh.

A revival of interest in traditional glazing methods and in glazed tiles in general occurred in the second half of the nineteenth century. Both medieval encaustic tiles (now machine-made) and hand-painted tiles were a feature of the decorative styles of the Aesthetic and Arts and Crafts movements, and later of Art Nouveau, with notable makers such as William de Morgan elevating the craft to an art form. A Moorish influence was evident, too: Leighton House in London is an outstanding example of exotic tilework dating from this period. Tiling still appeared as a common floor finish, particularly for kitchens and hallways, but tiles were increasingly seen as decorative embellishments. Cast-iron fire surrounds, for example, often featured flanking tiled inserts.

In the latter part of the twentieth century, tiling was valued chiefly for its practical advantages. In hot regions and in areas with strong tiling traditions, tiled floors and walls have long been a constant feature. But in more temperate areas, kitchens, but most particularly bathrooms, were generally the only rooms to be part- or wholly tiled, less for decorative effect than for ease of maintenance and water-resistance. Modern ceramic tiles, which have a uniform, rather neutral quality, particularly at the cheaper end of the market, have reinforced this practical image.

Nevertheless, that utilitarianism has more recently been challenged both by a growing interest in traditional handmade tiles – either plain terracotta or glazed – and by a new appreciation of the lustrous effect tiling can achieve. Tiling on the smallest scale of all – mosaic – has also seen a great revival and makes a surprisingly effective complement to contemporary fittings and fixtures.

brick & tile

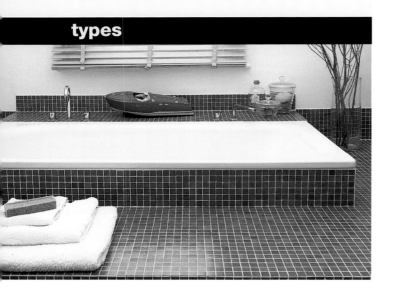

types

are more commonly understood to be those highly processed varieties made from refined clay.

Brick and terracotta tiles are not good conductors of heat, which means that they warm up more slowly and retain heat for longer than other materials. Terracotta tiles should be sealed before use. Quarry and ceramic tiles, on the other hand, make much colder, harder and more impervious surfaces.

Brick

Up until the mid-nineteenth century, bricks were all handmade, using raw materials derived from local deposits of clay. This resulted in an immensely characterful building material, with wide variations of colour and texture. Firing in wood- or coal-fuelled kilns produced further variations and slight imperfections of finish. Such irregularities contributed much to the liveliness of brick construction, a dimension that was lost after industrialization, when brick became a much more uniform and standardised product. There were many who regretted the change; the English architect Lutyens, who made a point of using local materials wherever possible, often specified handmade bricks for his buildings, bricks which were not only visually more dynamic but which were also narrower and longer than mass-produced varieties. Bricks are still made by hand today, but they are extremely expensive.

above **Mosaic is relatively non-slip, thanks to its tight grid.**

right **New brick makes a surprisingly contemporary looking background.**

Bricks and tiles vary considerably in strength and hence in their suitability for different applications. In the case of all ceramic products, including terracotta, strength is a function of the density of the clay, the type of glaze, if any, and the degree of firing. Only certain kinds of brick and tile can be used externally, while some types of glazing are more vulnerable to staining than others.

Technically, brick and all types of tile are 'ceramic' products, made by firing earth at high temperatures. 'Ceramic tiles', however,

Various grades of brick are now manufactured. Engineering bricks are made from unrefined clay that is pressed and burnt. These have good resistance to wear, frost, chemicals and impact. Brick paviors are made from refined clay and are fired at very high temperatures which means that they are exceptionally durable and waterproof; they can also be supplied with a non-slip texture. Paviors are thinner than standard bricks – they are 1.9cm (¾in) to 5.1cm (2in) in thickness, as opposed to 6.5cm (2¾in). Secondhand bricks, available from specialist suppliers or architectural salvage yards, can be more expensive than new bricks, depending on their condition.

Brick comes in a wide range of earthy colours, from pale salmon-pink through to purplish browns, the warm reddish palette being the result of iron in the clay. London stock bricks (the term 'stock' refers to an early method of hand-making) are yellow when new, mellowing to a greenish brown.

Handmade bricks (1, 2) are arguably the finest, but are relatively expensive. Stock bricks (3, 4, 5, 6) are a standard construction material. Weathered (7) and waterstruck (13) are textured. Wirecut (8, 9, 10, 11, 12, 14, 15) are extruded then cut by wire.

Terracotta tiles

Almost exclusively used as a flooring material, unglazed terracotta tiles have a warm, mellow appearance and a rustic appeal. They may be either handmade or manufactured, antique or new. Like brick, terracotta tiles are warm underfoot and can be exceptionally durable. They are, however, more demanding in terms of maintenance than other types of tile. They are porous and must be sealed before use.

Antique pammets between one and two hundred years old, reclaimed from barns, manor houses and chateaux, have an unbeatable depth of character. Many display the original tilemaker's marks on the reverse. Antique pammets and tiles are naturally limited in number and are correspondingly expensive. One of the rarest varieties is Antique Blanc Rose, which was not made after the nineteenth century and is found only in a small area of France. Parrefeuille tiles from southern France are more plentiful and, unusually, are rectangular in shape.

More affordable are new handmade tiles, produced in a variety of locations around the world, from Provence to Mexico, and made using traditional techniques and local deposits of clay. In some cases, this entails shaping the tiles by hand, leaving them to bake in the sun and then firing in a wood-burning kiln. The resultant irregularities of texture, colour and thickness contribute enormously to the appeal of the product. Different colours and textures are associated with different regions: yellow with Bordeaux, pale pink with Provence, deep red with Burgundy, ochre with Tuscany, and a warm orange with Mexico. Occasionally clays are blended which may produce a shading of tones across the surface of the tile. Flame marks and other variations of finish which result during firing only serve to enhance the liveliness of the surface. When new, terracotta has a leathery patina which deepens with age and use.

Handmade tiles tend to have a coarser texture than those that have been manufactured. Most machine-made tiles are more regular overall than the handmade ones, but computerized techniques can be employed to simulate the effect of old terracotta, so that no two tiles are the same in any given production run. Alternatively, machine-made tiles may be distressed to imitate the effect of a couple of centuries of wear. Terracotta tiles are available in a variety of shapes and sizes, including rectangles, octagons and the traditional 25-cm (10-in) square.

Glazed terracotta tiles are not as durable as their ceramic counterparts but they tend to be much more appealing, particularly the handmade and hand-glazed tiles. There is a wide range of colours, textures, patterns and styles, from traditional rustic tiles in solid vibrant colours and interpretations of blue-and-white Delft to contemporary pictorial or representational motifs. Finishes include high

Handmade terracotta tiles (1) and semi-handmade varieties (2) are produced in regions all over the world. Rather more practical, cheaper and easier to lay due to their regularity are simulated terracotta tiles (3, 4, 5, 6). Some machine-made terracotta tiles are artificially distressed.

gloss, satin, matt and metallic. Format is typically square, but rectangular tiles, some with bevelled edges, are also available, as are matching dados and borders made of tile. Depending on their composition and glazing, some types of glazed terracotta tiles are not suitable for use in showers or on kitchen worksurfaces.

Quarry tiles

Quarry tiles are the serviceable alternative to traditional terracotta and were first manufactured in Britain in the mid-nineteenth century. For those who are enamoured of vernacular handmade tiles, quarry tiles, with their slightly bland uniformity, make something of a poor substitute, but they have undoubtedly proved an extremely successful product.

Made from unrefined high-silica clays pressed into a mould and burnt, quarries come in a range of natural clay colours, including red, brown, and buff, as well as blue. Format is typically square and texture is slightly irregular. Quarries are relatively cheap, very durable and extremely wear-resistant, and can even be used externally if fully vitrified or high-fired.

Practicalities aside, quarries have a certain utilitarian image which can be less than appealing. Unlike terracotta tiles, they do not appreciably improve with wear giving them a rather lifeless quality.

Ceramic tiles

Ceramic tiles share the format and many of the applications of other types of fired earth but are highly processed products without the same degree of conspicuous authenticity. They are made from refined clay that is ground, pressed and fired at high temperatures. Some types are suitable for flooring or for cladding walls; fully vitrified tiles can be used outdoors. Ceramic tiles are widely available and range from cheap through to extremely expensive. Many of the highest-quality ceramic tiles come from Italy.

Practically speaking, ceramic tiles score high for durability, ease of maintenance, water- and stain-resistance. Disadvantages include the fact that they are generally cold, hard, heavy and can be slippery underfoot, particularly when wet.

The defining aesthetic characteristic of ceramic tiles is their regularity – a characteristic that enables them to be laid at fairly narrow spacings in even grids. In contemporary settings, this uniformity can be a positive asset, a degree of precision that works well where the emphasis is on crispness of detail. Since ceramic tiles do not age appreciably, their fresh, clean look will be maintained.

Another distinct advantage is the sheer variety of colours, textures, shapes and patterns on the market, everything from solid colour to pictorial motifs, from high gloss to matt, from embossed to

Hard-wearing and utilitarian quarry tiles come in a limited range of colours, typically red (1), brown (2) and black. One of the great advantages of ceramic tiles (3–6) is that they are available in a huge range of colours, textures and patterns.

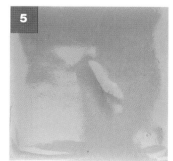

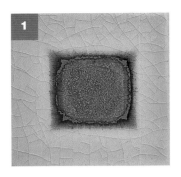

relief patterns. Dados, beadings, and other forms of edge trim and matching detail are also widely available. Ceramic tiles patterned with the aid of digital technology are an exciting new development. Designs range from crisp Op-art geometrics to hyper-realistic fruit, vegetables and other natural images taken from photographs scanned into the computer and transferred to tile.

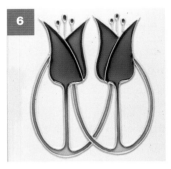

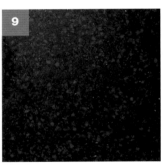
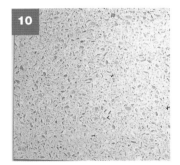

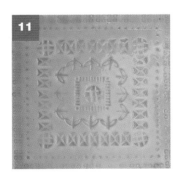

Tiles have been a vehicle for decorative art for centuries. Naive patterns and simple motifs are characteristic of handmade tiles, such as these examples from Mexico (3, 4). Contemporary techniques include using reactive glaze transfers in multiple layers (1, 2). Textured tiles are also a popular choice (11, 12, 13).

For a period look, there are embossed Victorian style tiles (5, 6) and tiles featuring traditional patterns or naturalistic designs (14, 15, 16). Plain tiles are also available in a range of colours (7, 8) and in fine porcelain (9, 10).

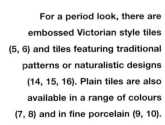

above **An integral skirting provides a neat finishing touch to a tiled floor.**

above **Digital technology has revolutionised tile design.**

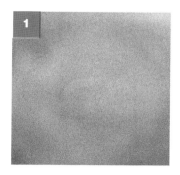

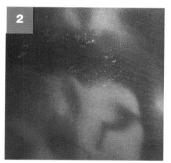

The most common types of ceramic wall tile are square in format, either 10.8cm (4¼in) square or 15cm (6in) square. Some have angled edges which meet flush with the wall so that the correct grouting space is left; others are supplied with plastic spacers. Edges may be straight and unglazed or curved and glazed so that no edge trim is required.

Contemporary ceramic tiles come in exciting textures and designs, including smooth metallic finishes (1, 2), textured metallic relief patterns (3, 4) and finishes simulating pewter (5, 6). Most spectacular are the new digitally produced designs derived from photographic imagery (7, 8, 9).

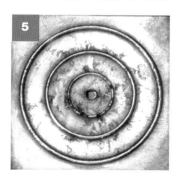

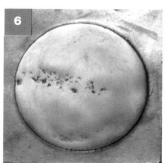

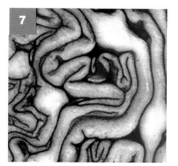

Encaustic tiles

Encaustic tiles are those where the design or pattern is inlaid rather than applied to the surface in the form of a glaze. The technique dates back to medieval times. At that period, terracotta tiles were stamped with a wooden block carved with a relief design while the clay was still damp and the impression was filled with white clay. The tiles were then glazed and fired. Typical designs included heraldic devices and Christian symbols – encaustic-tiled floors were often a feature of ecclesiastical buildings. Some tiles displayed individual motifs or designs; others were patterned so that a complete design was formed by a group of four or sixteen tiles.

The Gothic revival of the mid-nineteenth century saw a renewed interest in this form of decoration and encaustic tiles were put into mass production by Herbert Minton in Britain, from where they were exported all over the world. They became hugely popular and were a common feature of entranceways and porches in ordinary nineteenth-century homes. Many original encaustic-tiled floors still exist.

Designs from the nineteenth and early twentieth centuries are still manufactured for those who wish to recreate period decor, but there are also more contemporary designs on the market, featuring simple natural shapes and symbols. The technique of inlaying the semi-liquid material with differently coloured clay produces a matt tile with a certain softness of appearance. Some encaustic tiles are not made from clay, but of powdered marble and stone coloured

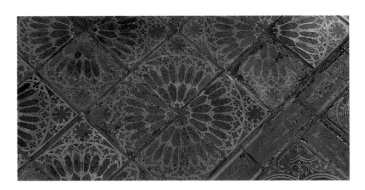

above **Original medieval encaustic tiles on the floor of the Chapter House, Westminster Abbey, London.**

with oxides. These are pressed rather than fired. Encaustic tiles can be used to create entire surfaces or as contrasting inserts within a plainer tiled ground.

Mosaic

Included in this section by virtue of its format, mosaic is tiling at the smallest scale. Individual *tesserae* or cubes of mosaic may be made of one of any number of materials: often of ceramic – glazed or unglazed – but equally of marble, stone, terracotta or vitreous glass. *Smalti* – handmade enamelled glass mosaics – are one of the most beautiful (and most expensive) mosaic materials. They have a superb depth and range of colour and a slightly uneven surface.

Some mosaics comprise only the naturally occurring colours of marble and stone – a nonetheless surprisingly vivid palette that includes pure blue lapis lazuli, brilliant green malachite and serpentine and a subtle range of neutral tones.

Ceramic and glass *tesserae* tend to be easier to lay than stone mosaic tiles since they are evenly dimensioned. For a high degree of authenticity and added definition, stone *tesserae* may be individually hand-cut on all four sides. Vitreous glass is not suitable for flooring applications because it fractures easily and is too slippery; similarly, to avoid slipperiness, honed marble *tesserae* should be chosen instead of polished marble for a floor mosaic.

Mosaic has an ancient history, dating back five thousand years. The Sumerians created mosaics using coloured clay pegs while the Egyptians combined similar materials with inlays of semi-precious stones. The Romans, however, were the first to cut stones into regular geometric shapes which they used to create beautiful mosaic pavements and panels, often depicting naturalistic themes. But it was the Byzantines who attained the peak of mosaic artistry. Hagia Sophia in Istanbul, which dates from the sixth century,

Encaustic tiles (1, 2) are through-patterned, which means that the design does not sit on top of the tile in the form of a glaze but is actually inlaid into the tile itself. The technique dates back to medieval times but was popularly revived during the nineteenth century.

features extensive glass mosaics, the glittering and richly coloured surfaces serving to dematerialize the solid walls and create a heightened sense of mysticism.

The enduring fascination of mosaic owes much to the fact that the eye constantly shifts between the detail of the individual pieces and the picture as a whole. At close range, mosaic can assume an almost abstract rhythm of colour and shape; at a distance, the many small elements that make up the design create a sense of softness and delicacy.

Mosaics that approach the intricacy and beauty of antique examples can be specially commissioned from mosaic artists who produce original designs for specific locations. Aside from the skill and artistic ability that the work entails, it is also exceptionally labour-intensive which means that one-off commissions are generally fairly expensive. Those enthusiastic amateurs who have had a little practice or who have learned the basics of the technique at a mosaic workshop or course can tackle less complex motifs and geometric patterns. At the very simplest level, mosaic tiling is available in sheet form backed either with netting or a peel-off paper so that surfaces can be covered quickly and easily. In this format, mosaic generally comprises either a single solid colour or a random arrangement of different shades. Either makes a striking contemporary backdrop for bathrooms and kitchens.

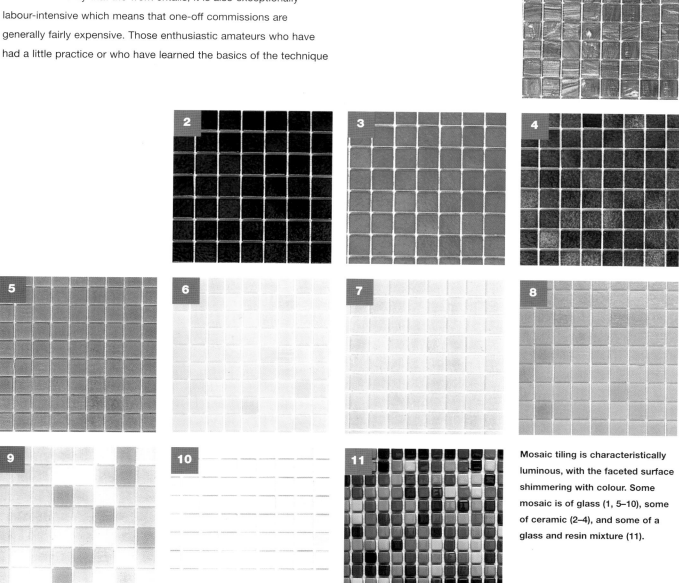

Mosaic tiling is characteristically luminous, with the faceted surface shimmering with colour. Some mosaic is of glass (1, 5–10), some of ceramic (2–4), and some of a glass and resin mixture (11).

applications

brick & tile

left **Black-and-white check tiling is a classic floor treatment. It is best to suit the scale of tile to the size of the room.**

right **A new brick wall framed in metal complements an existing wall stripped back to the original brickwork with supporting steel beams carrying the load of the upper floor.**

The typical applications of brick and tile arise from the physical and practical characteristics of this family of materials. Brick is chiefly used in construction, but serves well as a flooring material at ground level and can provide an evocatively textural backdrop when left exposed as a final wall finish. Tiles offer a range of practical advantages – good wear-resistance generally, and, in the case of glazed and ceramic tiles, water- and stain-resistance. In warm regions, extensive use of tiling on floors and walls helps to keep interiors cool.

The accessible format of brick and tile lends itself to the creation of pattern. Pattern can be as subtle as the repetitive manner in which individual elements are laid or as elaborate as the most sophisticated mosaic design. In between there are many effective and graphic ways in which contrasts of colour, texture and type can be exploited. Many of these have cultural or vernacular overtones: Provençal, Spanish, Mexican and Portuguese tilework have their own characteristic motifs and palettes, which may be echoed in manufacturers' ranges.

Working with tiles entails thinking about scale. In general, smaller tiles look better in more confined surroundings; larger tiles suit bigger expanses. The same is true of tile patterns. Very intricate or complex designs often look lost in a big space, while large, open, repeat designs require plenty of room.

applications

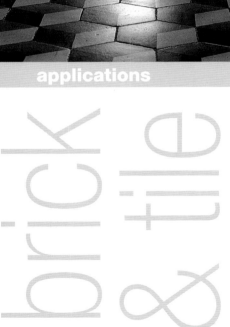

brick
& tile

flooring

Brick, tile and mosaic suitable for flooring are
fairly heavy materials, which may occasionally rule out their use on upper floors or over a
timber sub-floor. In all cases, a dry, rigid, level
base is required to minimise movement and
damp penetration, both of which can cause
individual elements to lift up. Only certain
types of brick and tile are suitable for outdoor
use. Those which are to any extent porous or
not fully vitrified will absorb moisture and be
prone to cracking in cold weather.

Brick has a naturally cosy, countrified
aesthetic and makes an unpretentious, warm
and welcoming floor in kitchens, entrances
and hallways, as well as in conservatories or
utility areas immediately adjacent to the

outdoors. But it is also good-looking enough to serve as a floor in informal sitting rooms and dining areas, where the rich earthy tones combine well with rugs or with natural fibre floor coverings.

Bricklaying is a considerable skill and should always be carried out by a professional. There are a number of traditional laying patterns, including herringbone, which has a strong sense of forward movement, basketweave, and stretcher bond, which is similar to the effect of walling.

far left **Tiles have the potential to age gracefully. This tiled floor, with its tumbling block pattern, dates from the early 1900s.**

left **The mosaic floor of this bathroom was inspired by Constructivist motifs.**

below left **A vivid mosaic floor with integral border has been laid directly over concrete.**

above **Ceramic tiles with their regular, even dimensions, complement clean modern lines.**

below **An antique terracotta floor in a period-style bathroom in Corsica.**

Bricks must be laid on a solid concrete sub-floor. A damp-proof membrane may be required between the base and the sand-and-cement mortar bed into which the bricks are laid. Grouting between the joints should be done immediately after laying. The joints themselves need to be wide enough to accommodate some shrinkage;

'movement' joints taken through to the bedding at intervals and around the perimeter, and which are topped with an elastic sealant, will reduce stresses in the floor which might be caused by changes in temperature or humidity.

Tiling suits areas of heavy traffic, such as hallways and corridors, as well as areas of the home where water- and stain-resistance is an asset, namely kitchens and bathrooms. The warm, earthy tones of terracotta and quarry tiles have a natural association with country settings; ceramic tiles have a cleaner and more contemporary appearance. Traditional tile patterns include the simple contrast of black-and-white chequerboard, the classical elegance of pale octagonals inset with small dark squares or diamond shapes, and plain tiled grounds inset with random glazed or encaustic feature tiles. In large areas, or at thresholds, more intricate designs, either geometric or pictorial, can provide a focal point or centrepiece. Borders accentuate areas of tiling and provide a neat finishing touch. In areas that are irregularly shaped, borders

brick & tile

look best inset from the perimeter rather than following the contours of the room.

Tiling requires a degree of skill and is probably best left to a professional, particularly if the tiles themselves represent something of an investment. Handmade tiles are generally uneven in thickness and require special care to install. Glazed tiles used as insets should be set lower than the main surface of the floor to protect the glazing from wear and abrasion. In the case of complex designs, dry-laying is recommended as a preliminary; this process can also help to minimize tile cutting and can accommodate irregular tiles by allowing for variation in the grouting joints.

Tiles are usually laid in either a mortar bed or are glued with proprietary adhesive and then grouted. The adhesive may be combined with an additive to promote flexibility; movement joints may also be advisable. In the case of unglazed terracotta, a little grout slurried across the surface during installation can provide a more authentically rustic appearance.

Mosaic floors represent the height of tiling art. Natural locations for mosaics include bathrooms and hallways – restricted areas where the sheer labour-intensiveness of the technique is not prohibitively expensive. Because each mosaic tile is so small, the grouting has a much greater impact on both the appearance and the performance of the final surface. In practical terms, grouting gives a mosaic floor a 'key' which reduces its slipperiness. Visually, the colour of the grouting can have an impact on the design. Matching light grouting with light-coloured mosaic, or dark with dark, makes the effect more seamless; contrasting grout, on the other hand, emphasizes the pieced nature of the effect and can be more graphic. A cement-based adhesive can be used either indoors or out.

The simplest way of laying mosaic is to use sheets of mosaic that are pre-stuck to a backing and to apply them in the same way as tiles. A variation of this method can be adopted to make mosaic pictures or patterns. It is done by sticking individual tiles face down on paper using water-soluble glue, grouting or slurrying the reverse of the tiles, and laying in place. Once the sections of mosaic are laid, the paper is wetted and peeled away before final grouting takes place. The most time-consuming method is to lay each mosaic tile

left **Bare brick walls make a rugged backdrop in a loft conversion.**

an existing feature – such as the lower edge of a window – to give coherence to the effect. Alternatively, you can finish the top edge of the tiling with a tiled moulding or border to suggest the effect of a dado.

Wall tiling can be tackled by an experienced amateur but if you are at all unconfident about your skills in this area the job is best left to a professional decorator.

far left **Mosaic contributes luminous colour.**

left **Practical ceramic tiles complement the porcelain sinks placed on an elm console.**

below **Small ceramic tiles frame the unusual feature of an inset fireplace.**

by hand in situ – be prepared for the floor to be out of commission for some consider-able length of time.

walls

The use of brick and tile on walls, like that of many other materials, tends to be most successful when it is wholehearted. If tiling has a dreary image at all, it is chiefly because it has often been restricted to the bare minimum – skimpy splashbacks behind kitchen or bathroom sinks, or a narrow border edging a bath. Tiling that ends at an indeterminate place midway up a wall, or is marooned in an expanse of plain plasterwork, always looks mean and ill-considered.

Whole tiled rooms, on the other hand, have an appeal of their own. Tiling an entire bathroom or shower creates a 'wet' room that does not need conventional enclosures or fittings since the water can drain directly to an outlet in the floor. In theory, almost any wall surface can be tiled; in practice, where the surface is curved or contoured, only the tiniest mosaic tiles will produce a smooth finish. If you intend to half- or part-tile a room, arrange the tiling so that it aligns with

from left to right **Full-height tiling looks more considered than stopping the tiles partway up the wall; brilliant blue mosaic forms a backdrop to a glass shower stall; blue, green and cream rectangular tiles are laid in a random pattern.**

below **The small scale of mosaic suits confined areas. For ease and speed, mosaic comes ready-to-lay in panels.**

below opposite **Mosaic in varied shades of pink with silver generates a sense of liveliness.**

Tiling, because it relies on straight lines and edges, is particularly intolerant of any lack of precision. Uneven wall surfaces can cause complications; tiles will also need to be cut and shaped to fit round obstacles such as pipework or windows.

Tiling can be applied to most wall finishes, including paint, paper, plaster and plasterboard, brickwork and even existing tiles. It is important, however, to ensure surfaces are dry and even; irregularities will show up in the final surface. There are a variety of different types of adhesives and grout on the market. Waterproof adhesive

applications

brick
& tile

far left **Mosaic made of Italian limestone has a soft luminous appearance.**

left **Bevelled white tiling has a retro appeal.**

tiles ideally should be fully vitrified so that they withstand cracking and exposure to heat. But no tile is completely damage-proof and tiled worksurfaces are prone to chip.

Thick tiles are not easy to cut and a stronger adhesive may be needed, as well as an epoxy-based grout. A certain amount of planning, cutting and shaping will inevitably be required to fit tiles around

should be used in wet areas; heatproof adhesive where tiles will be subject to high temperatures, such as behind stoves and cookers. Combined grout and adhesive is available which allows both sticking and grouting to be carried out in a single operation, but better results are usually achieved with separate grouting applied once the tiles have cured or set for about 12 hours.

Bare brickwork makes a lively, textural surface that gives warmth and depth of character in both rustic and contemporary settings. If you find the mellow tones of brick too dark and enclosing, the bricks can be painted to lighten the colour but at the same time retain the rhythmic quality of the surface. Non-structural applications involve the use of thin brick 'slips' which can be used as wall cladding to simulate the effect of brick con-struction. These are applied in a standard brick-bond pattern, stuck with adhesive and pointed with mortar, but they lack the strict authenticity of real brick construction.

worksurfaces

Tiles, particularly if they are intensely coloured, make a cheerful and attractive kitchen surface. A thicker grade of tile is required than those used for walls and the

applications

sinks, pipes, built-in hobs and other features. Place cut tiles towards the back of the worksurface so they are less noticeable.

other applications

Tile and mosaic can be used to cover almost any flat surface for decorative or practical effect. Table tops, window sills, mirror or picture frames and similar horizontal planes are ideal for small-scale tiling or mosaic. They are a good way for an amateur to get to grips with the techniques. Fragments of any type of ceramic or glass bedded in mortar can be used to create outdoor mosaic patterns, for instance as a decorative feature inset in a paved terrace or on a wall. Tiled inserts were a feature of nineteenth- and early twentieth-century washstands and cast-iron fire surrounds. Many salvage yards carry stock of originals.

The potential of brick is necessarily rather more limited. Any significant brick-built feature tends to have structural impli-cations due to the heaviness of the material. Brick surrounds can be constructed around fireplaces or built-in wall ovens provided they are resting on a solid concrete base.

care and maintenance

Provided the right type of brick or tile is chosen for the right use and location, maintenance is generally trouble-free. Tiles, especially glazed tiles, are most prone to damage during installation. Abrupt temperature changes may cause crazing; glass tiles or those with a metallic finish may be scratched during grouting.

Bricks and quarry tiles Newly laid brick and quarry tiles may show what is known as 'efflorescence' – deposits of white mineral salts on the surface. Repeated washing with water is required. Exposed brick walls and surfaces need little aftercare beyond occasional dusting. Brick and quarry-tiled floors can be cleaned by sweeping up loose dust and dirt and washing with warm water and a mild detergent. Thorough rinsing with clean water is necessary to avoid the build-up of soapy residues that can increase slip-periness and hold dirt.

Although standard bricks are highly porous and stain readily, sealing is not advisable. Non-porous quarry tiles and brick paviors can be very lightly coated with linseed oil, polish or seal to build up resistance to stains; over-sealing will make a floor dangerously slippery.

Unglazed terracotta These tiles are porous and require sealing before use as flooring. Many manufacturers supply tiles ready-sealed; if not, seal according to the recommended guidelines using a proprietary sealant or linseed oil and wax, and renew

top **Ceramic tiles can be cut to fit an unusual wavy-edged worksurface.**

centre **A patchwork effect has been created by decorating plain white tiles with ceramic paint.**

left **Bold ceramic tiles have been inset in a wooden table.**

above **Tiled splashbacks are practical, but grouting may need attention from time to time.**

the treatment at regular intervals. Sealing will deepen the colour of the tile and the burnished glowing patina should develop in about a year. Unglazed terracotta is particularly vulnerable to abrasion from tracked-in dirt, so regular sweeping is advised. Mop with warm water and mild detergent for routine cleaning.

Glazed terracotta Even with a glazed finish, terracotta tiles are still porous to a degree. Some varieties are unsuitable for use in a shower or on a kitchen worksurface. Tiles with a white or largely white glaze are more resistant to staining than those with a coloured glaze. Acidic foods and drinks can be very damaging. Avoid strong cleansers or harsh detergents, particularly when cleaning hand-glazed tiles.

Ceramic tiles Ceramic floor tiles are highly resistant to wear, staining and chemical attack and require little in the way of aftercare apart from routine mopping. Sealing is not required. If you want to polish ceramic tiles, apply polish sparingly and remove from time to time to prevent a build-up as this can become slippery and retain dirt.

Wall tiles Wall tiles are fairly impervious but

in time, dirt and wear tend to show up in the grouting. In extremely humid situations, grouting may grow mould which will need to be killed with a fungicide. Stained or dirty grout can be cleaned with mild detergent, using a small stiff brush, such as a toothbrush. Apply grout whitener after the surface has dried. If standard rather than waterproof grout has been used in a wet area, sections of grout may drop out. In this

case, it is best to rake out all existing grout and reapply using waterproof grout.

Old ceramic tiles sometimes display crazing, which can also be the result of damp. Crazed or damaged tiles cannot be repaired in situ but require replacement. Since tiles are produced in batches and colours may vary from batch to batch, it is always advisable to keep a few spare in case repairs become necessary.

Encaustic tiles The matt surface of these tiles is prone to staining, particularly during installation: handle with care. Encaustic tiles may be sealed. White areas naturally dull slightly with time.

Mosaic Mosaic used as a flooring should not be polished or the surface may become extremely slippery. Washing with a neutral detergent is generally sufficient for everyday cleaning.

below **Columns of thin red brick frame a fireplace.**

left **Concrete and plaster, materials that previously tended to be covered up with other finishes, are increasingly seen in a raw, unadorned state. Smooth plastered surfaces acquire greater depth of character when simply sealed to provide water-resistance.**

right **Bold, brash and a little brutal, concrete has a certain monumental quality that has its own beauty when sensitively lit.**

concrete &
plaster

right **Holes left by the casting process add surface pattern to a rugged concrete wall.**

left **A square aperture frames a view in the sweeping curve of a concrete internal wall.**

Concrete and plaster are composite materials made of similar natural ingredients that are readily available worldwide. Both are cheap, both are typically worked in a wet state and left to cure or harden, and both have been used in various forms for centuries. But whereas plaster is a traditional and reticent finish, concrete has long aroused quite astonishing degrees of invective.

This distinction is particularly marked when concrete and plaster are used indoors. Plaster, which is generally employed to make a smooth base for subsequent decoration, is one of the most self-effacing of all finishes. Concrete, on the other hand, thanks to its utilitarian and frankly rather brutal qualities, could not be more demonstrably avant-garde. Exposed concrete floors, walls and other surfaces announce a bold and uncompromising approach to interior design.

Despite a history that dates back to the Romans, concrete is firmly associated with modern architecture and even more strongly identified with conspicuous architectural failures of the urban landscape – failures conjured up by the phrase 'concrete jungle'. This is not altogether surprising. Firstly, the technological developments that enabled concrete to be used structurally rather than merely as an applied finish belong to the modern era. Secondly, while many well-loved and spectacular buildings have been made of concrete – the Guggenheim Museum in New York and the Sydney Opera House, to name but two – the cheapness of the material means that it has been widely used to create brutal and utilitarian structures, such as underground car parks and soulless tower blocks, which are difficult to regard as anything but eyesores. Between these two extremes are those concrete buildings that continue to inspire love and hate in equal measure, such as the South Bank arts complex in London.

In recent years, however, there are signs that the popular view of the material has softened somewhat. Trend-setting metropolitan interiors, featuring bare concrete walls and floors, have demonstrated that concrete can be handsome, monumental and as interesting texturally as stone. This shift of attitude owes a great deal to a change in the way plastered surfaces are now treated. The vogue for unpainted plasterwork, minimally sealed or waxed to create a warm and luminous effect, has restored a certain depth of character to a mundane material and, in the process, given people a taste for more robust styles of decoration. All in all, it is hard to conceive of a more robust treatment than bare concrete indoors.

The Romans, who were responsible for so many technological innovations in engineering and construction, were the first to make concrete and use it structurally. This discovery was lost with

left **Polished terrazzo makes a very elegant, sophisticated and hard-wearing floor. Its coolness underfoot is particularly welcome in hot climates.**

the fall of the Roman Empire and it was not until the Industrial Revolution that the material was, in a sense, rediscovered and its potential began to be explored.

Throughout the nineteenth century, concrete technology advanced in leaps and bounds. French engineers and architects were the first to grasp the principle of reinforcing concrete with metal rods or wire mesh and were the first to employ this technique in construction. Labrouste's Bibliothèque Sainte Geneviève in Paris, for example, made use of wire-reinforced plaster as early as 1845. 'Steel concrete' or 'ferro-concrete' was patented by another Frenchman, François Hennebique, in the 1890s and was dramatically exploited in the cantilevered design of his own house in 1904. The first architect to express concrete as a material in its own right was Auguste Perret. In Perret's Church of Notre Dame at Le Raincy (1922–3), windows consist of a trellis-like tracery of pre-cast concrete, echoing and updating the effect of stained-glass windows.

Concrete, both simple and austere, had a particular appeal for the designers of the Modern Movement. Its greatest advocate was undoubtedly Le Corbusier who made use of the material in many different idioms throughout his long and influential career. His early villas around Paris, with their smooth planes of pristine white-painted concrete raised up on reinforced concrete pillars (pilotis), defined a new modern aesthetic. Later buildings, such as the Chapel of Notre Dame at Ronchamp and the monastery of La Tourette at Eveux, reveal a more organic use of the material. At Ronchamp, concrete is used almost sculpturally to create soft sweeping curves, while the angled geometries of La Tourette are emphasized by the rough boarded concrete finish. The use of concrete was also integral to l'Unité d'Habitation in Marseilles, Le Corbusier's blueprint for social housing, and one of several similar projects.

While Le Corbusier succeeded in establishing concrete as one of the definitive materials of the twentieth century, he also unwittingly contributed to its eventual image problem. During the 1960s and 1970s, in many cities around the world, Le Corbusier's visionary approach to urban planning was put into practice by enthusiastic disciples of the International Style. Terraced streets and areas of substandard low-rise housing were cleared to make way for high-rise concrete tower blocks, raised on columns, and set in green space.

Unfortunately, many such projects were executed hastily and on the cheap, which meant that construction was often of a poor standard, a factor that eventually led to some dramatic structural failures. Facilities such as shared laundries, concierges, sports centres and shops, which humanized Le Corbusier's schemes and created a sense of community within individual blocks, were often left out of the equation on grounds of cost. Within a short space of time, both tower blocks and concrete-built estates had become new urban ghettoes, badly maintained and rife with vandalism and crime. It did not help that many of these concrete buildings were put up in parts of the world which did not enjoy a Mediterranean climate. In rainy weather concrete readily stains and under cold grey skies, it can look particularly bleak. Although few of the failures of the urban tower block, practical or aesthetic, are directly attributable to the inherent properties of concrete itself, the material has become a byword for some of the worst aspects of the contemporary environment.

Concrete's poor image has proved difficult to shake off, despite the fact that it has been used to create many

innovative and striking structures. In the United States, Frank Lloyd Wright made a particularly expressive use of the material, employing pierced and modelled concrete blocks to create an organic sensibility. At Fallingwater, completed in 1939, cantilevered concrete terraces projected over a waterfall spectacularly unite house with landscape.

In the latter part of the twentieth century, engineering advances allowed the material to be used as a thin shell and to be configured in every conceivable shape, from rippling wave-like forms to fluid spirals. A notable example, in this idiom, is the TWA terminal at John F. Kennedy International Airport, New York, designed by Eero Saarinen in 1962. The concrete roof of the structure, shaped like wings, encapsulates the excitement of air travel. Sydney Opera House by Jorn Utzon, at the entrance to Sydney Harbour, has a similarly dramatic profile. The nesting concrete shells of its roofline proved very complex to design and engineer. Because the concrete is covered in small white ceramic tiles, problems of discolouration have been avoided. A modern master of building in concrete is the Japanese architect Tadao Ando, whose work includes the Fabrica complex near Treviso in Italy and who values the material for its modesty and sculptural potential.

Unlike concrete, plaster has no real image problem; recently, it has barely seemed to have an image at all. Plaster has long been used, for both aesthetic and practical reasons, as an applied finish, both internally and externally (where the finish is known as 'render'). External plastering, which has been carried out since early times, generally consisted of a mixture of sand, lime and, later, of cement. Cement-based plastering, which came into fashion in the eighteenth century, was generally known as 'stucco' and was intended to simulate the effect of stonework. Very decorative external plastering was known as 'pargeting'; different patterns were often tied into specific localities. Many traditional plaster mixtures for external use were toughened with the addition of straw, horsehair and crushed terracotta. External

plastering increased weather resistance but it also had the effect of smoothing out rough surfaces. Typically the plastered surface would then be painted, usually with limewash.

Indoors, plaster has long been a finish for walls and ceilings, creating both a level surface for subsequent decorative treatment and providing a vehicle for embellishment in the form of mouldings, friezes, cornices and other types of architectural detailing. With the spread of classicism northwards from Renaissance Italy, such features were employed to subdivide the plane of the wall according to classical principles, replicating the proportions and features of a temple façade. In this way, the skirting at the base of the wall corresponded to the plinth of a column, with the frieze and cornice at the top comprising the entablature. In fine houses, decorative plasterwork might be commissioned from highly skilled craftsmen; by the eighteenth century, for more ordinary locations, such details were often available cast in moulds in workshops. The explosion of house building that followed the Industrial Revolution saw a standardization of these features and a corresponding decline in quality.

In the contemporary interior, newly plastered walls are typically minimally detailed, with few if any decorative mouldings. Smooth planes of plastered wall painted white or some equally neutral shade have provided the unexceptional and reticent backdrop to many modern interiors. But with increasing interest in country or natural finishes, 'raw' plasterwork has enjoyed a certain popularity. 'Raw' plaster, which may be sealed or waxed but which is not painted, has something of the effect of a frescoed surface, a rather urbane rusticity.

A material which shares some of the basic ingredients of plaster and concrete, but which has more refined and luxurious associations, is terrazzo. Either poured in situ or laid as tiles, terrazzo makes an elegant surface whose beauty is matched by high levels of wear-resistance.

concrete & plaster

above **A polished concrete floor makes a cool and surprisingly elegant background for a contemporary interior.**

right **As monumental as stone, but much less expensive, concrete has been used to create a robust vanity top and wall surface.**

The integrity of any concrete or plaster surface depends on the quality of the ingredients, the proportions of each ingredient and the skill of application. Laying concrete and plastering remain skilled operations and are not suitable for amateur experiment.

Concrete surfaces are hard and tend to amplify sound, particularly in the absence of soft furnishings or carpeting. They are also porous and if not sealed or finished, they stain readily. Concrete is fireproof and, when properly made, virtually indestructible. Like concrete, terrazzo is also cold, hard and noisy. Plaster forms a much softer surface, which is not proof against knocks or scrapes.

Concrete

The basic ingredients of concrete are cement, water and aggregate. For building purposes, the cement used these days is usually Portland cement, which is composed of limestone, aluminous clay, gypsum and silica. Aggregate consists of various mixtures of fine sand and coarser stones and gravel. Concrete is typically grey. Whiter concrete can be obtained by mixing white cement with pale aggregate.

The correct mixture has an important bearing on both performance and the integrity of the finish. If there is too little sand or too much water, the concrete will be less dense and will not be strong enough; if there is too much cement, cracking and shrinkage is more likely. Aggregate, which absorbs a great deal of water, lowers the density of the concrete.

Concrete sets in a matter of hours but takes up to a month to achieve maximum strength. The action of mixing water with cement instigates a chemical reaction which causes the concrete to harden. This process must take place at an even rate. Concrete will not set if it is mixed at or below freezing point.

For most domestic applications, concrete is either mixed and laid on site in the form of a sand and cement screed, or is used in the form of ready-made pre-cast slabs, tiles or panels. Another common or garden product is the concrete breeze block, mostly used to make internal and external partitions and cavity walls.

Reinforcement with steel rods, wire or mesh transforms concrete into a structural material. It is moulded into place by

above **A custom-made concrete wall panel reveals evocative textural variations.**

formwork, made of timber, plywood, metal or other materials. The surface quality of the formwork – smooth, grained or textured – leaves its characteristic imprint on the final concrete surface.

Recently, a new photo-etching technique has been developed that enables images and graphics to be transferred onto concrete fascia panels. Such custom designs are expensive, but the technique opens up the tantalizing possibility of a radical transformation in the aesthetic scope of the material.

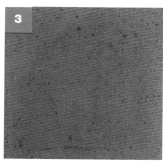

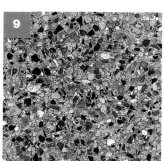

The image of concrete as a uniform, utilitarian material (2, 5) is belied by the range of colours and finishes, including acid-etched (1), polished (4, 10), diamond-rubbed (7, 8) and sealed with acrylic (6). Polished rough aggregate (9) gives a coarser look, while dyes can be added for colour (3).

Terrazzo

Terrazzo is a sleek and sophisticated material composed of an aggregate of marble, granite or coloured glass chippings, mixed with concrete or cement. Chiefly used as flooring, it can be poured in situ or laid in the form of tiles. Although terrazzo is most familiar today as a practical and hardwearing flooring treatment used in commercial interiors, it has been in domestic use in Mediterranean regions for many decades. The mixture of natural stones and marble results in a wide range of colours and patterns. Like concrete, terrazzo is exceptionally wear-resistant, especially when hydraulically pressed; unlike concrete, it is expensive.

Plaster

One of the basic ingredients of plaster for internal use is gypsum, a mineral which comes in a variety of colours, namely white, red, grey and yellowish-brown. Cement-based plaster, on the other hand, is designed for external finishes or for areas which are liable to damp.

There are different plasters on the market for different types of indoor use: undercoat plasters, plasters for finishing coats, plasters that can be applied as a single coat and renovating plasters for repair work. Important variables to consider include the porosity of the underlying surface and the ambient temperature at the time of plastering – both these elements will affect the rate at which the plaster sets. Plaster undercoats are suitable for absorbent surfaces such as brick; bonding undercoats for denser surfaces such as concrete. Acoustic plasters are available which incorporate sound-absorbing aggregate.

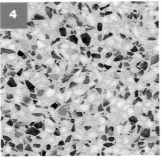

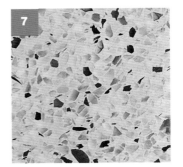

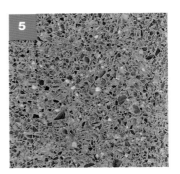

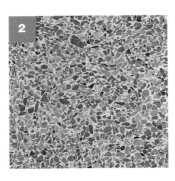

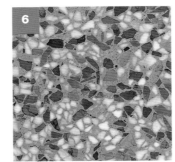

The appearance of terrazzo varies according to the size and type of material used in the aggregate. Larger chippings produce a more overt, open-pattern (3, 6) while finer chippings produce more of a flecked look (1, 4, 7).

Textured plasters, such as Artex, which result in a rough relief finish, have typically been used to cover up minor defects of the underlying surface. Such finishes, which are often worked in swirls or other patterns, may once have had a certain rustic appeal but the chief concern today is usually how to remove them. The answer is: with great difficulty. They can usually only be removed by hacking them off, which may well disturb what lies underneath. They can also be covered up with a skim coat of plaster but a bonding agent will need to be applied first so that the plaster adheres properly to the textured surface.

There are also various traditional recipes for ornamental plaster, the most notable of which is scagiola, a simulation of marble, which was often applied to pilasters and columns. Scagiola consists of plaster of Paris mixed with fragments of real marble, coloured cement and colouring agents dissolved in glue. It was applied over a rough lime and hair mortar, burnished with a pumice when dry, then rubbed with oil. To simulate veining, frayed pieces of string soaked in dye were impressed into the material while it was still workable. Once the surface set hard, the strings were removed and the crevices filled in.

above **Concrete steps make a minimal staircase cantilevered out from the wall.**

Plasterboard is commonly used over timber studwork and is subsequently finished, either by skimming with a fine coat of finishing plaster or by papering and painting. Most boards come with an ivory side for decorating and a grey side for plastering. Another type of plasterboard is thermal board, which has a backing of expanded polystyrene, and which is used as an insulator; some types incorporate a membrane between the board and the polystyrene which resists water vapour.

Plaster is a surface which is traditionally painted; more characterful results can be achieved by rubbing in pigment or adding pigment to the mix. The resulting shades are softer and more natural looking.

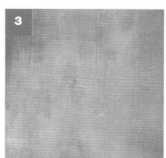

concrete & plaster

Concrete and plaster create integral interior finishes whose prime purpose has typically been to act as a level, even background for subsequent finishes. The idea of revealing concrete and plaster as material surfaces in their own right is relatively new.

By and large, the use of plaster is restricted to walls, ceilings and vertical planes such as columns or structural supports. Concrete, like terrazzo, is chiefly identified with flooring, especially at lower or basement levels.

flooring

The principal use of concrete in the domestic interior is as a sub-floor, providing a stable, even base for heavy materials such as ceramic tile, brick or stone. While older houses may have timber floors throughout, new construction tends to have concrete sub-floors, at ground level at least. Converted industrial or commercial buildings often feature concrete floors at every storey.

Exposed concrete has a rough, raw

aesthetic and a strong, sculptural quality: it is a material with considerable machismo. In practical terms, it is just as hard as it looks. Concrete floors make uncompromising surfaces, which are cold and noisy, and tiring to stand on for any length of time. Exposed concrete must be sealed to prevent the surface from dusting – breaking down into fine particles. Because concrete conducts heat well, it is suitable for laying over insulation and underfloor heating.

There are various ways of treating concrete which preserve its forthright appeal but at the same time knock off a few of its rough edges. Very uneven concrete surfaces can be finished with a smooth sand and cement screed which dries to a matt, suede-like texture. Alternatively, concrete can be surface-treated after curing by various mechanical means so that the finish acquires a burnished or polished look.

Special concrete paints and finishes, designed to provide tough and non-slip surfaces in factories and other industrial

concrete
& plaster

left **A simple mixture of white cement and sea sand makes a surprisingly attractive final floor in its own right, in sympathy with the contemporary furnishings.**

below **A number of proprietary toppings can be applied to concrete, including resin, which produces an exceptionally glossy, slick finish.**

settings, can be applied to concrete to provide both a jolt of colour and a less brutalizing texture. Acrylic or epoxy resin toppings, which are self-levelling and are designed to provide resistance to chemical attack, produce a glossy, lacquered effect that can be exceptionally sophisticated. These need to be laid professionally and may require some length of time to harden off fully.

Pre-cast concrete tiles tend to be associated with outdoor paving but the thinner varieties can be used indoors, provided the base or sub-floor can bear the weight. These are laid in the same way as

other heavy flooring materials such as ceramic tile and brick, by bedding in a mortar mix. Neat cement slurry must be applied to the backs of the tiles just before laying. After the mortar has set, joints are filled and pointed.

Terrazzo flooring, associated both with hot climates and commercial interiors, can be mixed and laid in situ or laid as tiles. Because the material is so heavy, in both cases it requires a level, solid concrete base. In the case of terrazzo laid in situ, the material is applied with a trowel within dividing strips made of brass or zinc. Once it has cured, it is ground smooth, any indentations are filled with cement paste and it is then polished. Tiles are laid in the same way as concrete tiles but rather than being separated by pointed joints, are often butted up in sections divided by metal strips.

concrete
& plaster

above **The appearance
of concrete is partly
determined by the type of
aggregate used in the mix,
as demonstrated by this
rough-textured concrete
stairway.**

left **Terrazzo tiles come
in a range of colours and
surface patterns. Large
stone chippings create an
overtly mottled effect.**

walls

Like concrete, untreated plaster is subject to dusting. Untreated, it is also particularly porous and prone to staining from greasy marks. For practical purposes, therefore, it is advisable to seal raw plaster in such a way as to preserve its appearance but provide a higher degree of impermeability. However, the problem with sealing, either with a matt varnish or wax, is that it tends to deepen the tone of the plaster considerably. This can be offset by rubbing white pigment into the plaster to lighten it beforehand.

Pinkish and pinkish-brown varieties of plaster are rather more appealing in an unfinished state than grey or off-white varieties. Their warm, mellow tones, which have the matt look of old frescoed walls and the depth of character of aged terracotta, make hospitable and naturalistic backgrounds, but should not be used in

above **Many modern structures are concrete-framed. Here, concrete beams and ceiling are exposed, giving a look of monumentality.**

left **Concrete is an incredibly strong material. These interconnecting planes, beams and supporting columns create a sense of sculptural play.**

areas of the home that are subject to excessive damp or humidity.

The standard finish for plaster is, of course, paint, which brings a huge range of colours into play. An equivalent colour choice but a more evocative final surface can be achieved by mixing powdered pigment into dry plaster before mixing. Once sealed, the finish retains a chalky, plastered texture but one which is saturated with an intense hue. Unusual textural effects can be created by adding particles of glitter, sawdust, straw or other fragments to the

concrete & plaster

left **A skim coat of plaster on a dividing wall serves as a bedhead. Plaster has a certain anonymity, which reduces the impact of such features.**

below left and right **Plaster comes in a range of shades from grey to pink, but pigments can also be added to the mix for more overt colour variation.**

mix, by impressing wet plaster with small pebbles or by scoring incised designs into the surface.

Converted factory buildings or warehouses may feature concrete walls as well as floors; for those particularly enamoured of the hard industrial aesthetic, any form of cosmetic concealment will be superfluous. Obviously, such rugged backgrounds have an uncompromising honesty which is part of their appeal; real devotees even find them sensual. Concrete panels can also be used as wall cladding indoors or to make solid partitions, provided the building's structure is sufficiently strong.

details

Being somewhat monolithic materials, concrete and plaster are not readily associated with interior detailing, except in the form of the traditional embellishments of cornicing, mouldings and ceiling roses typical of period decor. In the grandest sur-roundings, such details were often the work of highly skilled artisans; in the context of the ordinary eighteenth-, nineteenth- and early twentieth-century house, they were produced from pattern books. Today, ready-made plasterwork mouldings, cornices and ceiling roses are widely available in a range of traditional patterns, with those based on earlier designs tending to be more refined than the mid- to late-nineteenth-century ones. Similar features are also produced in polystyrene, and are naturally much lighter, cheaper and easier to install. Once painted, they are difficult to distinguish from the real thing. An alternative, if you are seeking to replicate original detailing or have sections of cornicing which are missing, is to commission an ornamental plasterer to make casts from existing fragments.

A word of caution: adding decorative plasterwork to contemporary interiors is

right **Vividly coloured concrete and render in the style of Mexico's best-known architect, Luis Barragán.**

below **A concrete divider separates a sleeping area from a dressing area in an open-plan space.**

above **Cement-lined sunken bath inset in a wooden floor.**

above **The suede-like appearance of this concrete bath adds character to a minimal bathroom.**

above **A simple concrete table provides a surface for outdoor eating.**

concrete & plaster

rarely a successful means of evoking a sense of the past. These details were proportional markers as much as they were architectural flourishes and today's rooms, with their lower ceilings, make inherently uneasy and unconvincing settings for such lavish effects.

A world away aesthetically, the humble concrete breeze block is a versatile product with a range of potential uses in the determinedly 'no-style' or utilitarian interior. Breeze blocks, like salvaged bricks, can be used to make rugged bases for table tops or supports for shelving, or can be built up into half-height or full-height partitions. The more blocks you use, however, the greater the weight and it is advisable to check the load-bearing capacity of the floor if you are embarking on a major interior construction.

Plaster is so readily abraded that its

practical use on horizontal surfaces is limited. One exception is shelving. Seasoned boards or salvaged timber can be given a light skim of plaster to obtain a bleached, rustic look.

care and maintenance

Both plaster and concrete require sealing to prevent dusting and to resist staining from oils. Plaster chips and scratches easily, hence the traditional protective skirting board and dado applied to portions of the wall most likely to be bumped and scraped. It must be thoroughly dry before subsequent finishes can be applied.

Major defects in plasterwork are likely to be indicative of underlying structural faults, such as subsidence or other forms of movement. Hairline cracks are normal, but cracks which are wide and which continue to widen mean that further investigation is required.

Major defects in concrete surfaces, particularly those laid in situ, tend to be the result of a poor initial mix or inadequate curing. Very soft or powdery concrete surfaces often mean that too much water has been absorbed in the mix by the aggregates, while mixes that are overly rich in cement often craze. In high temperatures, concrete must be protected during curing to prevent water evaporating at too fast a rate and resulting in stresses in the material.

Concrete and terrazzo can be maintained by scrubbing with detergent and hot water. Rinse soap off thoroughly. Mild scouring powder will tackle engrained dirt. Terrazzo should not be polished or it will become dangerously slippery.

right **Unfinished concrete walls make a rugged surface for a bathroom and are a stark contrast to the lightness and transparency of the rest of the room.**

below **Terrazzo is an unexpected but beautiful and durable worksurface in a kitchen.**

synthetics, leather & linoleum

synthetics, leather & linoleum

left **Plastic is a thoroughly modern material, with a huge range of applications. These ribbed plastic panels make effective and lightweight room dividers.**

right **Shiny PVC plastic curtaining used as a screen separates a kitchen area from the rest of the living space, multiplying reflections.**

left **Plastic is increasingly favoured by contemporary furniture designers. The curvy Bluebell chair, designed by Ross Lovegrove, has a plastic shell and is available in three colours.**

right **Studded rubber makes a hard-wearing floor. One particular advantage of the material is that it is available in a huge range of brilliant colours.**

This final grouping straddles the great material divide. Plastic is demonstrably synthetic; leather and linoleum are purely natural in composition. Plastic is a thoroughly modern material, the product of twentieth-century advances in the petro-chemical industry; linoleum dates back nearly a century and a half, while the use of leather goes back to time immemorial. What these three materials do have in common, however, is that they lack the cultural frames of reference that come from structural applications. Unlike stone or concrete, timber or steel, which are strongly identified with different building types, the associations that plastic, leather and linoleum bring to the interior largely arise outside architectural or engineering contexts.

The first fully synthetic plastic was invented just under a century ago by a Belgian chemist called Leo Baekeland. Bakelite (phenol formaldehyde) was only available in one colour – dark brown – and was very brittle, a factor which limited its applications. Bakelite is probably best known today as the material used to make early radio cabinets, telephone handsets, and desk equipment, retro associations that have invested it with a certain degree of charm and collectability.

The two great leaps forward in plastics technology occurred in the aftermath of the two world wars. During the 1920s and 1930s, acrylic, polystyrene, nylon, polyethelene and PVC (polyvinylchloride) were invented, as well as associated production techniques such as injection-moulding. At this stage, however, the applications of plastic were only beginning to be explored and it was not until after the Second World War that plastic finally came of age.

At this point, when oil replaced gas in the manufacture of plastics, the number of different types of plastic multiplied enormously – polypropylene, for example, was first developed in 1953. Overall quality and performance also saw a marked improvement from the 1950s onwards and new forming techniques broadened the applications of this family of materials beyond all recognition.

right **Semi-opaque ribbed
plastic provides a degree of
privacy while allowing light
through. Plastic is much
lighter than glass and safer
for such applications.**

Few materials have infiltrated our lives to such an extent as plastic – or in such a short space of time. Ordinary household paint is largely plastic; plastic can also be found in seals, varnishes and resins commonly used as protective coatings for floors. There is plastic in laminated countertops, melamine kitchen units and vinyl flooring; in light fittings, shower curtains, switches, plugs, lavatory seats, computer housings, toys, utensils, containers, bins, and packaging. A huge proportion of the most basic household products, fittings and fixtures in everyday use are either wholly or significantly plastic. At the same time, while there may not yet be a definable plastic 'architecture', plastic has such a huge range of applications in building – from fibreglass and acrylic panels, to pipes and tubing, insulation and window frames – that such a distinction almost ceases to be relevant.

What lies behind this revolution is partly economics – plastic is inexpensive – but it is principally due to the nature of plastic itself. Plastic is the ultimate 'designer' material in that it can be precisely engineered to meet specific performance requirements. The fundamental characteristics of wood, for example, set certain limits that determine its use; with plastic, it is the other way round – the use determines the type of plastic. Plastic can be soft, bendable, rigid, transparent, opaque, translucent, coloured, patterned and processed into an infinite number of shapes and forms. It is small wonder that it has become such an entrenched part of our existence.

If concrete, another defiantly modern material, often inspires loathing, our seemingly irreversible dependency on plastic often induces a sense of guilt. Plastic is so cheap that its use has been inextricably bound up with the throwaway culture of excessive consumerism – a world in which we routinely discard mountains of non-biodegradable plastic packaging and 'disposable' plastic products with little apparent thought of the environmental consequences. The oil crisis of 1973 – which temporarily sent plastic prices rocketing – was the first stern reminder of what such consequences might be and, ever since, plastic has been widely regarded as the definitive non-environmentally friendly material. This reputation has only been consolidated when, from time to time, studies are published apparently indicating potential health risks caused by long-term exposure to plastic-based products and finishes.

If the use of plastic arouses a certain unease on ecological and health grounds, its aesthetic qualities also inspire a degree of ambivalence. Early plastics were difficult to colour and did not perform particularly well; in addition, they were often used as a cheap simulation of real materials, such as stone, plaster and timber. The result is that plastic has gained a reputation for shoddiness, superficiality and dishonesty. Compared with many materials, plastic is lightweight and, unlike natural materials, it does not acquire any depth of character with age and use – factors that also serve to reinforce its poor image.

There has, however, been something of a turnaround in our appreciation of its aesthetic qualities in recent years. Part of the reason is simply that plastic has now been around long enough to inspire retrospective affection; modern classics in plastic by designers such as Verner Panton and Joe Columbo dating from the 1960s and 1970s routinely sell well at auction. Where plastic has been used more robustly, notably in thicker sections, it has also acquired more

left **Vinyl is a form of plastic used to make cheap and cheerful floor coverings. Vivid colours and simple patterns are often more successful than vinyl designed to simulate real materials such as wood and stone.**

right **Leather is one of the most sumptuous of all materials. Here it has been used to cover a door and wall, with the stitching overtly expressed to emphasize tactility.**

of the status of a material in its own right – many chunky and glossy 1960s kitchen and household products displayed a sense of quality and substance. Conversely, plastic's image gained a massive boost from the development of a translucent type of polypropylene in the mid-1990s. This brought a more tactile dimension into play and enabled colours to be purer and somewhat luminous. Plastic has always had its enthusiasts, but mainstream approval may finally be on its way.

Although there remain many environmental concerns about the use of plastic, a certain amount of reassessment in this area has also taken place. Plastic can be recyled very successfully; carrier bags and other types of plastic packaging have been transformed into striking plastic sheet and panels that can be jointed to make furniture or applied like cladding. The fact that designers such as Philippe Starck are positively choosing, on environmental grounds, to create products in plastic rather than deplete timber stocks still further, has broadened the debate.

We might, with great difficulty, learn to wean ourselves away from the convenience and practicality that plastic offers, but it might also be surprisingly hard to forego its aesthetic advantages. If we could imagine a world without plastic, it would be a world that was considerably less colourful than it is today. Bright colour has always been available for the wealthy in society, but it took the development of plastic to bring every shade in the spectrum into ordinary homes. Because it can be bent, shaped and moulded in any conceivable fashion, it has enabled designers to

experiment with new, more expressive forms. The problem with plastic may ultimately lie not in its inherent characteristics, but in the way we choose to use it.

In many ways plastic's polar opposite, leather, is a supremely luxurious and extravagant material for interior surfaces and finishes. It is highly expensive and, of course, utterly natural. While leather upholstery is very much an established part of the decorating repertoire – hides and skins have been used for centuries as covers for seats and back rests – the use of leather as a flooring and cladding material is relatively new on the interior design scene. Price alone is enough to maintain the exclusivity of this material, but for those who can afford it, leather surfaces and finishes have an unbeatable sensuality and a depth of character that matures with time.

Linoleum, a material chiefly employed as a floor covering, was once viewed as negatively as plastic is today. Invented in the mid-nineteenth century, and widely used as an affordable substitute for tiling, in recent years it has shaken off its dreary between-the-wars association with hospital corridors, thanks to an improved manufacturing process and the availability of a wide range of vivid colours and patterns. Like plastic, linoleum's image has suffered somewhat from the fact that it has often been patterned to simulate other more worthy materials – so much so that many people still believe it to be a synthetic. Unlike plastic, however, linoleum is an entirely natural product with many environmental credentials.

synthetics, leather & linoleum

types

above **Plastics can be formed into many shapes, as demonstrated by this rippled magazine rack made of acrylic.**

Types of plastic

Plastics are created by a process known as polymerization, which involves joining together many individual molecules (monomers) to form a chain (polymer). There are three main types of polymer: thermoplastics, thermosets and elastomers.

Thermoplastics, which are made of long-chain polymers, include the flexible plastics polystyrene, polythene, polypropylene, PVC, acrylic and nylon. These plastics can be formed into very complicated shapes and are quite sensitive to variations in temperature. They become soft when heated and stiff when cooled, and heating and cooling can be repeated indefinitely.

Thermosets, made of cross-linked polymers, include the rigid plastics polyester, melamine and silicone. They, too, become soft and malleable when heated, but once they have set they cannot be softened again. Thermosets have better fire-resistance than thermoplastics and are stronger.

Elastomers, formed of coiled chains of polymers, have the unique ability to regain their shape after stress. Synthetic rubber is a good example of an elastomer.

Plastics as a whole are flammable and, once alight, they not only burn rapidly but also give off toxic fumes. The softer plastics, notably PVC, are also associated with 'off-gassing' – the release of chemical vapours into the atmosphere. Other plastics, including formaldehydes, are known irritants and have been identified as one cause of a range of health problems.

Types of thermoplastics

Acrylic The best known acrylic is perspex, available in sheet form and widely used as a substitute for glazing. Acrylic is also used to make shower cubicles, baths and sinks. Transparent acrylic sheet is lighter and resists breakage better than glass, but it is more expensive and flammable and it scratches easily, which can make it less transparent.

Polythene This thin plastic film, familiar in packaging, is commonly used to insulate outdoor cables and provide a protective coating for metals.

PVC (polyvinylchloride) PVC has a huge range of applications, from damp-proof membranes to shower curtains and floor finishes. Vinyl floor tiles and sheeting are made of PVC while inflatable furniture and pop objects, such as the 'Blow' chair, are made of heat-welded PVC. PVC has a short lifespan, especially when exposed to ultraviolet radiation. It also attracts dust.

Polypropylene New, more translucent forms of polypropylene in pure luminous colours have helped transform the image of plastic as a whole. One famous polyprop design is Robin Day's ubiquitous stacking chair, designed in 1963 and still in production; more recently, chairs by Philippe Starck make elegant use of the material. Designer ranges of household objects, such as laundry bins, toilet brushes and dustpans, are now produced in brightly coloured polypropylene.

above **These cork-backed photographic tiles are covered with a layer of PVC to promote wear- and moisture-resistance.**

Polystyrene Most familiar as protective packaging, polystyrene is also used to make pre-formed covings and simulated plasterwork detailing. In foam form it is a common component of furniture.

Polycarbonate Applications of polycarbonate include glazing and a variety of household goods. It is more expensive than acrylic but also more scratch-resistant.

Nylon Technically a polyamide, nylon gains its name from the twin centres of its development, NY-LONdon. Best known as a fibre employed in inexpensive carpet, nylon is also used to make door furniture and curtain rails.

Polyvinylacetate This is a common ingredient in emulsion paint, floor finishes and adhesives.

Teflon (PTFE or **polytetrafluoraethylene)** is a non-stick material first developed as a protective coating for panels on spacecraft. Domestic applications include coatings for kitchen utensils and saucepans. Teflon can also be used to coat fabrics and increase their weather-resistance: the roof of the Millennium Dome in London comprises panels of PTFE-coated fibreglass.

Types of thermosets

Melamine Melamine has been used extensively to create a wide range of decorative laminates for worksurfaces, countertops and similar applications.

Polyurethane This type of polyester has the ability to form a hard film in a short space of time, which gives it widespread application in paints and varnishes. Foamed polyurethane is used in insulation and as the lining of cushions and mattresses. It is also employed as an underlay or as a core material in panels and fascia boards. Polyurethane is one of the plastics associated with health risks and can cause respiratory difficulties. It is very combustible.

Polyester resins (Fibreglass [GRP]) is made by combining glass fibre with polyester resin.

Epoxy resins These materials have very strong properties of adhesion and are used to make coatings and very tough glues. They have some toxic elements.

Formaldehyde is commonly used as a preservative or bonding agent in a wide range of household goods, including furnishing fabrics and carpeting and manufactured wood products such as hardboard, chipboard, plywood and particle board. It has been shown to act as an irritant to skin, eyes, nose and throat and can cause respiratory ailments, headaches, fatigue and nausea.

Ureaformaldehyde is found in glues and floor seals. Once commonly used for cavity-wall insulation, there has been concern about health risks and its use is now banned in some countries.

below **Plastic applications in the home are almost limitless. These storage units are both cheap and easy-care.**

Formica

A popular trade name that has passed into generic use, Formica encompasses various types of high-performance laminated panels commonly used as decorative and practical surfaces for tables and countertops. Patterns include simulations of wood, metal and stone, together with a wide range of abstract designs and solid colours. Traditional Formica is constructed from layers of paper impregnated with thermosetting resins, bonded under high pressure and heat. Thicker varieties with solid cores are also available, as are laminates that are coloured throughout.

Corian

Another trademarked product, Corian comprises a blend of acrylic and natural minerals which form a solid material available in a range of thicknesses. Corian can be cut, sculpted, drilled and worked into countertops, sink units and a host of other similar domestic and commercial applications. One particular virtue is that it is through-coloured, so patterns and colours do not wear away or de-laminate. Corian does not off-gas at normal temperatures and is non-toxic and hypo-allergenic. It resists heat, impact, stains and fire and is available in over 90 colours.

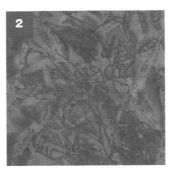

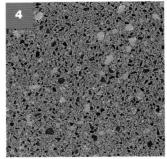

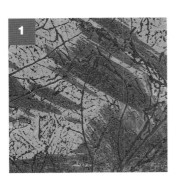

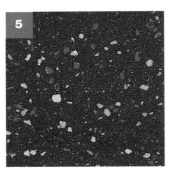

Laminates come in a huge range of colours, patterns and simulated finishes, including metallic relief (1) and smooth metallics (2). Corian (3, 4, 5) is a unique product with a wide range of applications. Corian is coloured throughout which means that any surface damage can be sanded out.

Vinyl

Synthetic flooring products, such as tiles and sheet, all contain some proportion of PVC. The higher the percentage, the better the quality and performance; the best vinyl is, accordingly, as expensive as some natural materials. There is a huge range of colours, textures and patterns on the market, with a certain bias towards the simulation of natural materials such as stone, terracotta and wood.

Vinyl is waterproof and resists most household chemicals as well as grease. It is not resistant to cigarette burns, however, and is extremely flammable. Various grades and thicknesses are available and the thinner tiles or sheets do not wear well. Bleach and strong cleaning products can discolour the material, as can rubber heels. Resilience and insulating qualities can be increased by backing or cushioning with an interlayer of foam.

above **A Corian worksurface with inset drainage grooves. Corian can be worked in a variety of ways, including drilling and sculpting.**

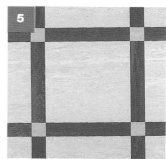

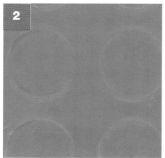

Vinyl ranges from the cheap to the expensive, depending on the thickness and PVC content. These examples are all studded with relief patterns to increase slip resistance (1, 2); extra slip-resistant safety flooring (3).

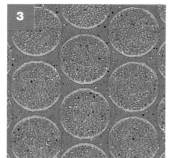

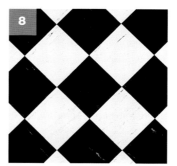

Although mass-market vinyl flooring is dominated by simulations of natural materials, simple geometric patterns are generally far more effective (4, 5, 6, 7, 8).

Synthetic rubber

Demand for natural rubber far outstrips supply so most rubber used in interiors today – in the form of rubber floor tiles or sheeting – is made of vulcanized synthetic rubber, silica and pigment. Synthetic rubber is much easier to colour than natural rubber. It is a very high-performance product, incredibly wear- and slip-resistant and totally waterproof. It is also anti-static, anti-bacterial, resistant to cigarette burns, and has good sound-insulation properties. Rubber that is oil- or grease-resistant or which is suitable for outdoor use can be made to order. Modern synthetic rubber is available in a huge range of colours, textures and finishes, including marbled or terrazzo effects.

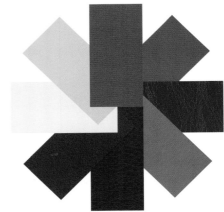

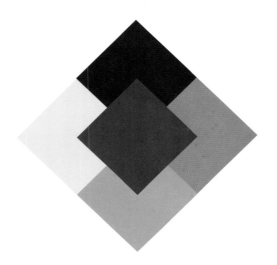

Leather

Leather used in upholstery and clothing is a particularly sensual material – soft, supple and with a wonderfully evocative smell. Many of these same qualities are present in leather floor and wall tiles, but these are rather more robust. For such applications, steer hide, taken from the central section of the hide where the fibres are toughest, is used. The leather is then cured by vegetable tanning and coloured with aniline dyes. Tiles come in a variety of sizes and shapes and in warm, rich colours including russets, dark red, natural browns, dark green and black.

Leather makes a surprisingly hard-wearing surface and is warm, resilient and sound-absorbent. Although scratching is unavoidable in flooring applications, with regular maintenance the material acquires a rich patina.

Many types of rubber are relief-textured to promote slip-resistance (1, 2, 3, 4), with dots, studs, lozenges or treadplate patterns. Although flooring and cladding leathers are chiefly available in rich, natural shades, colour choice is broader for upholstery leather (5, 6, 7).

Linoleum

Linoleum was invented in 1863 by the Englishman Frederick Walton. Its name derives from *oleum lini*, or linseed oil, a by-product of flax. Although linoleum is widely perceived as a synthetic, it is an entirely natural product composed of linseed oil, pine resin, powdered cork, wood flour, powdered limestone and pigment. The raw mixture is pressed onto jute or hessian, left to dry for several weeks and then baked at a high temperature. The result is a smooth material with a matt, granular appearance; even brightly coloured linoleum retains a certain natural softness. Pre-war linoleum was rather brittle and tended to crack with wear and age. The introduction of vinyl after the Second World War saw a rapid decline in linoleum's popularity, a trend dramatically reversed in recent decades now that technological improvements have increased the range of colours, patterns and textures that can be achieved. Contemporary linoleum is a material of some robustness and sophistication and is fairly expensive.

Linoleum's practical advantages are considerable. It is naturally anti-bacterial, which makes it an ideal surface for kitchens and family rooms, and which has also led to its widespread use in hospitals and clinics. It is also anti-static, repelling the dust that attracts house-dust mites, and is therefore recommended for households where there are asthmatics or others suffering from allergic reactions. Warm, quiet, comfortable and fairly non-slip, today's linoleum matures with age and actually gets tougher as time goes by.

above **Many companies specialise in custom designs in linoleum, such as this decorative shell centrepiece.**

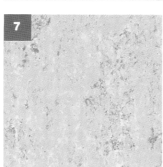

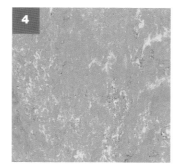

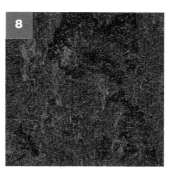

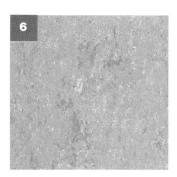

Because linoleum is composed entirely of natural ingredients, colours tend to be softer than for equivalent plastic-based products. The colour range (1–8), however, is very wide.

applications

synthetics, leather & linoleum

left and right **The double-layered rubber floor of this New York apartment belongs to a dancer who often uses the space as a rehearsal area. A firm rubber floor overlays interlocking tiles of spongy rubber.**

Synthetics perform many useful behind-the-scenes functions in the interior, as seals, varnishes, paints and protective coatings, as foams and linings, and in the prosaic form of ordinary fixtures and fittings, such as pipework, light switches, sockets and plugs. In such contexts, practical performance is almost the sole issue, although in recent years environmental and health risks have increasingly come into sharper focus. The more overt use of plastics brings aesthetic factors into play.

If plastic often seems to lack a specific aesthetic of its own, to a large extent that is because it has so often been called upon to mimic the decorative qualities of natural materials. Ever since Bakelite stood in for wood in early radio cabinets, plastics have been used to simulate glass, marble, stone, timber, terracotta, terrazzo and other traditional surfaces. At the top end of the market, such simulations can be very convincing indeed, at least visually; at the lower end, simulated surfaces advertise their lack of authenticity as soon as you set eyes on them.

Yet simulation in decoration has a long and worthy history. For centuries, wood and plaster have been painted, grained, stippled and veined to suggest all kinds of exotic and luxurious materials without causing the slightest unease. In the case of synthetic simulations, however, part of the difficulty is that plastics often appear curiously content-free: surface is all. The fact that they do not resonate sensually – we tend not to revel in their smell or texture – means that they have little physical presence. This may account for the fact that synthetic simulations can be such an immediate let-down when you touch them or walk on them. They have

undoubtedly delivered the superficial attraction of 'real' materials for those who could otherwise not afford them, or for those who find that the maintenance natural materials often entail is ultimately off-putting. But if plastics have any kind of beauty at all, it is more likely to be apparent when they are used for their own sake.

What various types of plastics do have to offer is strong, vivid colour and an irreverent, kitsch quality that can be usefully employed to cut through the rather high-minded seriousness of the modern interior. The all-synthetic interior – a Space Age fantasy of the 1960s – would be a truly alienating environment, but the occasional synthetic surface or detail combines practicality with a certain contemporary flair.

flooring

Vinyl, rubber, leather and linoleum floorings are lightweight, relatively easy to install and form seamless surfaces with no obvious joins. Although leather floors have to be pieced, vinyl, rubber and linoleum are available as sheet as well as tiles. Sheet increases the sense of visual unity. All these types of flooring are generally comfortable, warm, resilient underfoot (with the exception of the cheapest grades of vinyl), and fairly easy to maintain. The principal practical difference between them is that vinyl is generally not as long-lasting nor does it improve or acquire any depth of character with use. A worn synthetic floor has little charm to speak of.

Vinyl flooring is a popular mainstream choice, especially for areas of the home such as kitchens, bathrooms, halls, and playrooms, all of which require a high level of water-resistance. Although vinyl flooring

above **Perspex shelving makes a practical alternative to glass. The floor is linoleum over blockboard. Lino is particularly desirable in the kitchen as it has anti-bacterial properties.**

right **Blue rubber flooring in a kitchen area. The raised texture prevents slipping but requires extra maintenance to prevent a build up of grime.**

above **New vinyl-faced cork tiles come
in a range of photographic designs,
including this stone print.**

left **Glossy blue lino makes a good-looking
and practical kitchen floor.**

keeping with contemporary interiors. Bright,
graphic colours and abstract textural patterns
such as speckling, streaking or marbling
provide instant uplift without any of the
'dishonest' overtones of the look-alike
ranges. For the ultimate in floor-level reality,
manufacturers produce witty photographic
tiles that include fallen leaves, pebbles,
sunlight dancing on water, sandy beaches
and grass. The tiles are backed in cork and
sealed with a thick layer of PVC laminate.

Modern linoleum offers an equivalent
colour and pattern choice. Textural effects
include marbling, flecks and mottling;
geometrics such as plaids, stripes, tumbling
blocks and keystones are also available.
Computerized cutting can be used to create
very intricate one-off inlaid designs to order,
with or without integral borders.

Before laying, linoleum needs to
acclimatize in situ for a period of about 48
hours. The sub-floor must be perfectly
smooth, even and dry. Linoleum tiles should
be butted up tightly together to prevent

can be laid over almost any existing surface,
it is important to ensure that the sub-floor is
free from unevenness or protrusions which
will cause the vinyl to wear through in
patches. This may entail, for example,
covering existing floorboards with a layer of
hardboard. Vinyl is available in a wide range
of different sized and shaped tiles and in
sheets up to 4m (13 ft) wide. In either format
it is secured with a proprietary adhesive and

is easy enough for the skilled amateur to
install.

Aesthetically speaking, the choice of
vinyl flooring is vast, from upmarket
simulations to cheap and cheerful colour and
pattern ranges. More robust synthetics
designed for retail or commercial use often
incorporate sparkly granules or quartz flakes
to increase slip-resistance. These have an
attractive, glittery appearance that is well in

damp from penetrating the joints; the tiles will subsequently expand rather than shrink as time goes by. Sheet linoleum is heavy and unwieldy and requires professional installation; seams need to be hot-welded and the surface rolled perfectly flat.

Rubber flooring – one of the elements borrowed from industrial and commercial contexts – was a common accompaniment to high-tech-style interiors. Incredibly tough and wear-resistant, it retains something of that hard, technical edge, particularly the relief-patterned designs. The colour range is vast, with the emphasis on bold, contemporary shades; some manufacturers even guarantee to colour-match any internationally recognized colour reference. Surfaces include smooth (available in solid colour, marbled or terrazzo finishes) and a wide range of relief patterns, such as studded, ribbed, treadplate and gridded. These textured floorings, designed to increase slip-resistance, also have a tendency to collect dirt and may be more difficult to clean. The best quality rubber is thicker than standard and more expensive. Tiles and sheet are easy to lay; the sub-floor should be dry, smooth and even. Adhesive is applied to both sub-floor and flooring and the two surfaces are brought together after a specified period.

Leather flooring is sumptuous and surprisingly practical, apart from in wet areas such as kitchens and bathrooms. A truly original flooring choice, leather suits a wide range of interior styles, from classic to contemporary; its rich mellow tones combine well with other natural materials and with East-West fusion decorating schemes. The sheer sensuality of leather flooring comes at a price; if you can afford it, however, when properly maintained, leather is long-lasting. Tiles are tightly butted up and stuck with contact adhesive. The sub-floor must be dry, level and even, and preferably covered with hardboard or

synthetics, leather & linoleum

left **Linoleum, an entirely natural material, comes in a wide range of colours and patterns. This burnt orange lino floor has a soft, glowing appearance.**

right **Leather used as wall cladding is supremely tactile. Here the effect is enhanced by concealed downlights.**

plywood. Any gaps due to irregularly shaped tiles can be filled with carnuba wax.

walls and worksurfaces

Laminates such as Formica and other synthetics like Corian make ideal surfaces for hard-working areas in the home. These highly processed materials are available in a range of sizes, shapes and thicknesses, with the thicker varieties more commonly used for horizontal applications and the thinner suitable for wall cladding. The more expensive high-performance synthetics deliver considerable practical advantages and are easy to maintain; at the lower end of the market, resistance to heat, scrapes and cuts will be considerably less. Some synthetics are

below **A patchwork of leather makes an unusual yet durable floor in a converted warehouse.**

used to make integral sinks or hand basins; stone-effect sinks are considerably lighter and easier to maintain than the real thing but are disconcertingly warm to the touch.

Many of these materials are produced in simulation of wood, metal and stone – with varying degrees of success. More abstract patterns or textural effects can be more effective. Manufacturers have recently woken up to the appeal of strong colour and their bright shades provide a good way of adding an accent of vitality.

Laminate panels can be used to clad any vertical surface, as splashbacks or decorative fronts for kitchen and vanity units, or as simulated wood panelling for larger expanses. Less obtrusively, Perspex can also provide a water-resistant background for kitchen and bathroom areas, but it should not be used near sources of heat, such as behind cookers.

At the opposite end of the materials spectrum, leather wall tiles add an intimate sense of enclosure to the interior: they are ideal for cladding the wall behind a bedhead, perhaps, or to introduce a clubby note to a study alcove. Some artists have also been experimenting with inlay techniques to create abstract wall panels made of linoleum; once sealed, these are fully waterproof.

applications

far left **Recycled plastic, made from bottles, containers and bags, can be used to make worktops and furniture.**

left **Backlit Perspex panels provide colourful illumination along the length of a hallway.**

below **Translucent plastic screens framed in wood provide lightweight internal divisions.**

far right **Synthetic materials are often patterned to suggest the real thing. This acrylic basin surround resembles granite.**

right **A ribbed plastic wall painted bright green resembles corrugated iron.**

opposite, below **Plastic has gained an upmarket image from its use in innovative designs, such as this light by Ingo Mauer.**

synthetics, leather & linoleum

furnishings and fittings

The current fashionability of the retro home, borrowing heavily from the 1960s onwards, has brought synthetic furnishings and fittings once again to the fore. Part Pop, part kitsch and part garage-sale-chic, plastic products have a certain tongue-in-cheek appeal. This retro trend has seen the re-emergence of such classic designs as the inflatable chair in see-through PVC and Robin Day's all-purpose Polyprop chair, together with new designs for household objects in pure luminous colour. Collectable junk, such as 1950s saucer chairs made of woven plastic strips, broaden the frame of reference.

A similar theme can be pursued with all kinds of accessories – from plastic bead curtains and fluttering multi-coloured doorway strips to vibrant Zulu baskets woven out of plastic-coated telephone wire. At floor level, strips of Astroturf or plastic runners make vibrant additions; Perspex screens and window shutters have a crisp, contemporary appeal. What counts in this context is the deliberate material choice; unlike mundane synthetic household goods which are generally as unlovely as they are practical, modern synthetics make a virtue of their material use.

Leather, of course, needs little introduction as a furnishing material and is in wide use as upholstery for sofas and chairs. Low-level leather- or suede-clad cubes strike a more contemporary note; try leather curtaining for the ultimate in chic sophistication.

care and maintenance

What synthetics seem to promise, above all, is easy maintenance. When it comes to the upper price ranges and the best quality, this

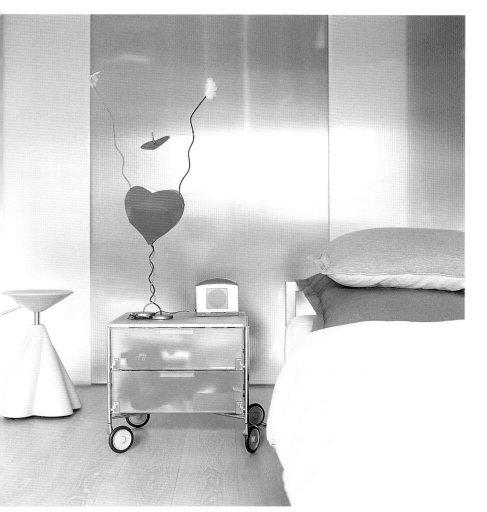

applications

synthetics, leather & linoleum

is, by and large, true. Very high-quality vinyl flooring and synthetic surfaces are designed for optimum performance and will take any amount of punishment. Lower down the scale, overall resistance to wear, chemical attack and, most critically, to fire, decreases

left **Leather has long been a popular choice for seat upholstery; these modern chairs update the use of the material.**

below **The arrival of plastics allowed designers to experiment with new, fluid forms, as demonstrated by the seamless moulded shell of a 1970s French recliner.**

opposite, below **See-through Perspex chairs add a futuristic dimension to the interior.**

dramatically. Very cheap synthetics have the briefest of lifespans.

Vinyl flooring There is no need to seal, but you should avoid the use of abrasives or bleach-based detergents which can cause discolouration and premature wear. Black marks from rubber heels will stain permanently if not tackled immediately. Other sources of damage include tracked-in grit, stiletto heels, cigarette burns, solvents and nail-polish remover. Care should be taken to avoid dragging heavy objects across the surface.

For general maintenance, wash with mild detergent and rinse well. Polish with a water-based polish if required, although this may increase slipperiness to an unacceptable degree.

Linoleum flooring After laying, some colours (particularly white, grey or blue) may show a yellow tint known as 'stove yellowing'. This is a temporary discolouration, the result of the maturing process, and disappears after a few hours' exposure to daylight – or a few

above **An original 1950s laminate-topped table has retro appeal.**

left **Laminate – cheap, practical and available in a range of colours and textures – is a common finish for cupboard fronts, worksurfaces and other forms of cladding.**

weeks', in the case of poorly lit areas such as basements.

No sealing is required. For a glossy look, apply emulsion polish and buff up. Dust or vacuum to remove loose dirt and debris; for heavy soiling, use a damp mop and mild detergent, but avoid over-wetting. Permanent damage can be caused by solvents, washing soda and oven cleaner. Cigarette burns can be rubbed away.

Rubber flooring Remove any surface dusting with a special cleaner. Rubber can be left matt but polishing sparingly with a water-soluble polish provides added protection. Clean regularly with a damp mop and mild detergent and always rinse well.

Leather flooring Leather should be regularly waxed, which feeds the leather and will also serve to provide basic moisture-resistance. After laying, the floor should be waxed and buffed at least three times before it is walked on. Thereafter, it will require buffing every fortnight and waxing every six months.

Synthetic worksurfaces Performance and maintenance vary considerably, according to quality. Water and mild detergent should be used for routine cleaning; avoid harsh abrasives such as scouring powders and acid-based cleaners. Excess heat can also be a problem; protect surfaces with trivets or mats when setting down hot cookware. Some cheaper laminates are readily damaged by cigarette burns and are prone to show scuffs and scratches. Except in the case of Corian, which is non-porous, strong solutions may stain permanently.

index

acknowledgements

The publisher has made every effort to trace the copyright holders, architects and designers and apologises in advance for any unintentional omission. They would be pleased to insert the appropriate acknowledgement in any subsequent edition.

1 top Patrick McLeavey/Griffon Joinery; 1 above Ozone Glass Limited; 1 centre Deralam; 1 below Dalsouple; 1 bottom Patrick McLeavey/Pallam Precast; 2 *Marie Claire Maison*/Gilles de Chabaneix/Catherine de Chabaneix; 3 Richard Davies/architect Philip Gumuchdjian; 4 Undine Pröhl/architect Enrique Norten; 5 Undine Pröhl/architect José de Yturbe; 7 Minh & Wass Photography/designer Tyler Hays; 8 Red Cover/Ken Hayden; 10-11 Richard Glover/architect John Pawson; 12 Richard Davies; 14 *Marie Claire Maison*/Gilles de Chabaneix/Catherine de Chabaneix; 15 View/Chris Gascoigne/architect Simon Condor; 16 Christian Sarramon/architect Marc Corbiau; 17 Red Cover/James Merrell; 19 Verne Fotografie/architect Bataille & Ibens; 20-21 *Marie Claire Maison*/Alexandre Bailhache/Catherine Ardouin; 22-23 Michael Moran/architects Moneo Brock; 24 above Alexander van Berge; 24 (1,3,4,5,6) J Crispin & Sons; 24 (2) Patrick McLeavey/Griffon Joinery; 24 (7) Hemisphere/Solid Floors; 25 above Maralyn Roberts Communications/ Mark Wilkinson Furniture; 25 (1-5) J Crispin & Sons; 25 (6) Patrick McLeavey/Griffon Joinery; 25 (7) Hemisphere/Solid Floors; 26 (1,2,3,5,6) J Crispin & Sons; 26 (4) Hemisphere/ Solid Floors; 26 (7) Patrick McLeavey/ Griffon Joinery; 27 above James Harris/architect Ushida Findlay; 27 (1,2,4,5) J Crispin & Sons; 27 (3) Patrick McLeavey/Griffon Joinery; 28 above Victorian Wood Works; 28 (1, 3, 4, 5) Lassco; 28 (2) Paul Ryan/International Interiors/designer Jacqueline Morabito; 28 (6) Victorian Wood Works; 29 above The Interior Archive/Henry Wilson; 29 (1-5) Patrick McLeavey/Griffon Joinery; 30 above www.elizabethwhiting.com/ Friedhelm Thomas; 30 (1-4) Siesta Cork Tile Company; 31 Narratives/Jan Baldwin/architects Melocco & Moore; 32 Paul Ryan/International Interiors/designer Gordon de Vries; 33 James Harris/ architect Ushida Findlay; 34 above left The Interior Archive/Henry Wilson/ architect Voon Yee Wong; 34 above right Richard Davies/architect Spencer Fung; 34 below *Marie Claire Maison*/Antoine Bootz/Billaud/Rozensztroch; 35 left View/Chris Gascoigne/architects Cogswell Horne; 35 right Richard Glover/architect Arthur Collin; 36 above Richard Glover/designer Jeremy Slater; 36 below Richard Glover/designer Malin Iovino; 37 Paul Ryan/International Interiors/architect Jacob Cronstedt; 38 left Red Cover/Graham Atkins-Hughes; 38 right James Harris/architect Ushida Findlay; 39 above The Interior Archive/ Simon Upton/London Interiors/designer Ou Baholydin; 39 below Paul Ryan/ International Interiors/architect Moneo Brock; 40 above Richard Glover/Reading & West Architects; 40 below Alexander van Berge; 41 above Verne Fotografie; 41 below Richard Glover; 42 left Verne Fotografie/architect Vincent van Duysen; 42 right Alexander van Berge; 43 *Marie Claire Maison* Maison/Antoine Bootz/ Billaud/Rozensztroch; 44 Richard Glover/architect John Pawson; 45 Red Cover/Winfried Heinze/architect Mark Guard; 46-47 Red Cover/Ken Hayden/architect John Pawson; 48-49 The Interior Archive/Inside/Michel Arnaud; 50-51 The Interior Archive/Henry Wilson/architect John Pawson; 51 Ray Main/Mainstream; 52 above Christian Sarramon; 52 below View/Chris Gascoigne/Alan Power Architects; 53 above Wentworth Communications/ Burlington Slate; 53 (1-7) Kirkstone; 54 above Patrick McLeavey/Fired Earth; 54 (1-5) Patrick McLeavey/Marble Flooring Specialists Limited; 55 above Richard Glover/designer Jeremy Slater; 55 (1-6) Kirkstone; 56 above Kirkstone; 56 (1-8) Kirkstone; 57 left www.elizabethwhiting.com/Andreas von Einsiedel; 57 right Stonell; 58 above *Maison Madame Figaro*/Gilles Trillard; 58 (1) *Maison Madame Figaro*/Gilles Trillard; 58 (2-4) ARC PR/Paris Ceramics; 59 above Patrick McLeavey/Stonell; 59 below Patrick McLeavey/Kirkstone; 60-61 Lanny Provo/designer Dennis Jenkins; 62 Paul Ryan/International Interiors/ architects Barnes & Coy; 62-63James Harris/architect Ushida Findlay; 63 The Interior Archive/Eduardo Munoz/architect Nico Rensch; 64 left Richard Davies/ architect Darren Gayer; 64 right Camera Press/*Sarie Visi*/Ryno/architect Arthur Quinton; 65 above Paul Ryan/ International Interiors/architect Barnes & Coy; 65 below The Interior Archive/ Inside/Michel Arnaud; 66 Deidi von Schaewen; 67 above left Paul Ryan/International Interiors/architect Deborah Berke; 67 above right Narratives/Jan Baldwin; 67 below Verne Fotografie/architect John Pawson; 68 above Richard Davies/architect John Pawson; 68 below left David Spero/ architect Seth Stein; 68 below centre Alexander van Berge; 68 below right The Interior Archive/Henry Wilson/architect John Pawson; 69 Geoff Lung/architect Renato d'Ettorre; 70 Arcaid/Geoff Lung/*Belle*/Stephen Varady Architecture; 71 MooArc/Andy Wilson; 72-73 *Marie Claire Maison*/Alexandre Bailhache/ architect Jacques-Emile Lecarron; 73 *Marie Claire Maison*/Gilles de Chabaneix/Catherine Ardouin; 74-75 Verne Fotografie; 76 above Tim Street-Porter/MAURICE TUCKMAN; 76 below View/Chris Gascoigne/Alan Power Architects; 77 above & centre Arcaid/Richard Bryant/architect Seth Stein; 77 (1-3) Patrick McLeavey/ Macmillan Stained Glass; 78 Paul Ryan/International Interiors/designer Jacqueline Morabito; 79 above Red Cover/Verity Welstead; 79 (1, 3, 6) Patrick McLeavey/Macmillan Stained Glass; 79 (2, 4, 5) Ozone Glass Limited; 80 above Fusion Glass Designs Limited; 80 (1-7) Patrick McLeavey/Macmillan Stained Glass; 81 above Ray Main/ Mainstream; 81 (1-3) ©IPC Syndication; 82 The Interior Archive/Henry Wilson/ architect Ian Chee; 82-83 Richard Davies/architect Darren Gayer ; 84 left The Interior Archive/Henry Wilson/ architect Justin de Silas; 84 right Christian Sarramon/designer Fabienne Villacreces ; 85 left *Marie Claire Maison*/Marie-Pierre Morel/Marie Kalt; 85 right View/Dennis Gilbert/architect Chance de Silva/artist Matt Hale; 86 left View/Chris Gascoigne/Alan Power Architects; 86 right Ray Main/ Mainstream/architect Simon Condor; 87 left Christian Sarramon; 87 right The Interior Archive/Ed Reeve/architects Adjaye & Associates; 88 above Paul Ryan/International Interiors/architect Pierce & Allen; 88 below Houses & Interiors/Verne Fotografie/architects Bataille & Ibens; 89 above Verne Fotografie/architect Geert Clarysse; 89 below Undine Pröhl/architect Jim Jennings; 90 above Ray Main/ Mainstream/C2 Architects; 90 below The Interior Archive/Henry Wilson/architect Ian Chee; 91 above Paul Ryan/ International Interiors/designer Charles Rutherfoord; 91 below left Red Cover/Jake Fitzjones/designer Fulham Kitchens; 91 below right Paul Ryan/International Interiors/architect David Ling; 92 Narratives/Jan Baldwin/ architects Melocco & Moore; 93 View/ Peter Cook/architects The Tugman Partnership; 94 The Interior Archive/ Inside Stock Image Production/Ryno; 95 Geoff Lung/architect Ed Lippmann; 96 Narratives/Jan Baldwin/architect Pierre Lombart; 97 Red Cover/Ken Hayden; 98 Paul Ryan/International Interiors/architect Paul Pasman; 99 Minh & Wass Photography; 101 The Interior Archive/ House & Leisure/architects Godsell Associates, Melbourne; 102 above Arcaid/Richard Bryant/architect John Young; 102 below Red Cover/ Trevor Richards; 103 above www.elizabethwhiting.com/Rodney Hyett; 103 (1, 2) Bragman Flett; 103 (3, 4) Forgetec; 104 above Arcaid/Richard Bryant; 104 (1, 2, 3) Deralam; 104 (4, 5) Bragman Flett; 105 above The Interior Archive/Fritz von der Schulenburg; 105 (1) The Interior Archive/Fritz von der Schulenburg; 105 (2, 3) Deralam; 106-107 View/Dennis Gilbert/architects Child Graddon Lewis; 108 above left Alexander van Berge; 108 above right Undine Pröhl/architects Scogin Elam Bray; 108 below Red Cover/Ken Hayden; 109 Verne Fotografie/architect Jo Crepain 110 above *Marie Claire Maison*/Marie-Pierre Morel/Catherine Ardouin; 110 below Richard Davies/architect Robin Snell; 111 above left Alexander van Berge/ designer Annemoon Geurtsen; 111 above right *Belle*/Andrew Lehmann/ architect Clive Lucas, Stapleton & Partners; 111 centre Paul Ryan/ International Interiors/architect Peter Romaniuk; 111 below David Spero/ architect Seth Stein; 112 above left *Marie Claire Maison*/Gilles de Chabaneix/Daneil Rozenztroch; 112 above centre Christian Sarramon; 112 above right Alexander van Berge; 112 below Paul Ryan/international Interiors/designer Michael Seibert; 113 left Richard Waite/architects Found Associates; 113 right The Interior Archive/Herbert Ypma/architect Deamer Phillips; 114 left The Interior Archive/ Henry Wilson/architect Mark Guard; 114 right Richard Davies/architects Brookes Randall Stacey; 115 Verne Fotografie/ architect C Zapolta; 116 The Interior Archive/Ed Reeve/designer Ou Baholydin; 117 Pavel Stecha/architect Joze Plecnik; 118-119 View/Dennis Gilbert/architect Chance de Silva; 120 The Interior Archive/Edina van der Wyck; 121 *Marie Claire Maison*/Gilles de Chabaneix/ Catherine Ardouin; 122-123 *Marie Claire Maison*/Nicolas Tosi/Catherine Ardouin; 124 left Ray Main/Mainstream; 124 right www.elizabethwhiting.com/Rodney Hyett; 125 (1-15) Ibstock Brick Limited; 126 (1-6) Patrick McLeavey/World's End Tiles; 127 (1-6) Patrick McLeavey/ World's End Tiles; 128 (1-6, 14-16) Patrick McLeavey/Fired Earth; 128 (7-13) Patrick McLeavey/World's End Tiles; 129 above left Christian Sarramon; 129 above right Dominic Crinson Digitile; 129 (1, 2) Patrick McLeavey/Fired Earth; 129 (3, 4) Patrick McLeavey/World's End Tiles; 129 (5, 6) Tantrum; 129 (7-9) Dominic Crinson Digitile; 130 above Collections/Malcolm Crowthers; 130 (1, 2) Patrick McLeavey/Fired Earth; 131 (1-11) Patrick McLeavey/World's End Tiles; 132 Christian Sarramon; 132-133 Richard Davies/architect Andrew Thompson; 134 above left Taverne Fotografie Agency/Hotze Eisma; 134 above right *Marie Claire Maison*/Marie-Pierre Morel/Catherine Ardouin; 134 below Taverne Fotografie Agency/Hotze Eisma; 135 above The Interior Archive/Ed Reeve/designer Ou Baholydin; 135 below *Marie Claire Maison*/Gilles de Chabaneix/Catherine Ardouin; 136 Red Cover/Andreas von Einsiedel; 137 above left Houses & Interiors/Verne Fotografie; 137 above right Richard Davies/architect Spencer Fung; 137 below Undine Pröhl/architect Ettore Sottsass; 138 above left Christian Sarramon; 138 above centre Richard Glover/designer Malin Iovino; 138 above right Red Cover/Verity Welstead; 138 below Verne Fotografie; 139 above left Andreas von Einsiedel/interior designer Sophie Stonor; 139 above right ©IPC Syndication; 139 below Pieter Estersohn; 140 above Ray Main/Mainstream; 140 centre *Marie Claire Idées*/Gilles de Chabaneix/ Catherine Ardouin; 140 below Ray Main/Mainstream; 141 above Robert Dye Associates/Richard Powers; 141 below Tim Street-Porter/architect Richard Neutra/designer John Solomon; 142 View/Chris Gascoigne/architects John Kerr Associates; 143 Geoff Lung/ architect Ed Lippmann; 144 Paul Ryan/ International Interiors/architects Hariri & Hariri; 144-145 The Interior Archive/ Inside Stock Images Production/*House & Leisure*/Dook; 146 Undine Pröhl/architect Donald Wexler; 148 Paul Ryan/ International Interiors/architect Peter de Bretteville; 149 Mark Seelen/designer Winka Dubbledam; 150 above Red Cover/Winfried Heinze; 150 below www.elizabethwhiting.com/Tim Street-Porter; 151 above Paul Davies Design/IMAI restaurant, Osaka, 1986; 151 (1-2, 4-8, 10) Patrick McLeavey/ Paul Davies Design; 151 (3 & 9) Patrick McLeavey/Pallam Precast; 152 (1-7) Patrick McLeavey/Pallam Precast; 153 above Geoff Lung/architect Dale Jones-Evans; 153 (1) *Marie Claire Maison*/Gilles de Chabaneix/Catherine de Chabaneix; 153 (2) Undine Pröhl/ architect Geary Cunningham; 153 (3) www.elizabethwhiting.com/Tom Leighton; 153 (4) Undine Pröhl/architect Legorreta Arquitecto; 154-155 David Spero/ architect Caruso St John; 156 left Camera Press/Sarie Visi/Ryno; 156 right Adjaye & Associates; 157 Ray Main/ Mainstream/architect Sergison Bates; 158 above Verne Fotografie; 158 below Trevor Mein; 159 left Ray Main/ Mainstream/architects McDowell & Benedetti; 159 right Paul Ryan/ International Interiors/architect Deborah Berke; 160 above Undine Pröhl/architect Geary Cunningham; 160 below left www.elizabethwhiting.com/Tom Leighton; 160 below right www.elizabethwhiting.com/Andreas von Einsiedel; 161 above Undine Pröhl/ architect Legorreta Arquitecto; 161 below Camera Press/*Sarie Visi*; 162 left Christian Sarramon; 162 centre *Eigenhuis & Interieur*/Hotze Eisma; 162 right Verne Fotografie; 163 left Guy Obijn; 163 right Taverne Fotografie Agency/production Frank Visser/Mirjam Bleeker/architect Bernardo Gomez-Pimienta; 164 Ray Main/Mainstream/ Sapcote Lofts; 165 Ray Main/ Mainstream; 166 *Marie Claire Maison*/ Eric Morin/Catherine Ardouin; 167 Dalsouple; 169 *Marie Claire Maison*/ Claude Weber/Prudhome-Bene; 170 Solvi dos Santos; 171 Modus PR/Bill Amberg; 172 Ray Main/Mainstream/ Ozwald Boateng; 173 above Articulate Communications/Harvey Maria; 173 below Guy Obijn; 174 above left Perstorp; 174 above right Sheila Fitzjones Consultancy/Corian; 174 (1, 2) Deralam; 174 (3-5) Sheila Fitzjones Consultancy/Corian; 175 above Sheila Fitzjones Consultancy/Corian; 175 (1-3) Jaymart; 175 (4-8) First Floor; 176 above left Dalsouple; 176 above right Bridge of Weir, Fine Scottish Leather; 176 (1-4) Dalsouple; 176 (5-7) Bridge of Weir, Fine Scottish Leather; 177 above The Interior Archive/Jonathan Pilkington; 177 (1-8) Forbo Nairn; 178 Minh & Wass Photography/architect Pierce & Allen; 178-179 Paul Ryan/International Interiors/architect Pierce & Allen; 180 above Paul Ryan/International Interiors/ designer Nick Dine; 180 below Arcaid/ Richard Bryant/architect Stirling & Gowan; 181 left Ray Main/Mainstream/ designer Malin Iovina; 181 right Ray Main/Mainstream; 182 *Marie Claire Maison*/Marie-Pierre Morel/Catherine Ardouin; 183 above Modus PR/Bill Amberg; 183 below Paul Warchol/ Blackstock Leather; 184 above left Ray Main/Mainstream; 184 above right Ray Main/Mainstream/architect Sergison Bates; 184 below Minh & Wass Photography/designer Patrick Marchand; 185 above left Undine Pröhl/architect Natalye Appel; 185 above right Richard Glover/Mance Design & Architecture; 185 below Guy Obijn; 186 above Arcaid/Richard Bryant/D'Soto Architects; 186 below Guy Obijn; 187 above left Arcaid/Richard Powers; 187 above right Arcaid/Alberto Piovano/architect Mariano Boggia; 187 below Guy Obijn.

Author's acknowledgements

I would like to thank Alison Cathie, Ann Furniss and Mary Evans at Quadrille; Paul Welti and Nadine Bazar; and particularly Hilary Mandleberg for keeping the book on course.

Wood

Atelier du Chêne Ltd
Grange Lane, Whitegate, Winsford,
Cheshire CW7 2PS
Tel: 01606 861442
Oak, elm, ash, maple, walnut in long and wide boards

Bruce Hardwood Floors (UK) Ltd
9 Moorbrook, Southmead Industrial Park, Didcot, Oxon. OX11 7HP
Tel: 01235 515100
Fax: 01235 817220

J. Crispin & Sons
92-96,Curtain Road,
London EC2A 3AA
Tel: 020 7739 4857 /
020 7739 2131
Fax: 020 7613 2047
Veneer merchants and importers

Finewood Floors Ltd
Suite F5, Skillion Business Centre,
1 Hawley Road, London N18 3BP
Tel: 020 8884 1515
American oak, English oak, walnut, cherry, ash, maple, European and American elm; solid wide-plank floors, parquet and chevron patterns

Forest Stewardship Council
Unit D, Station Building, Llanidloes,
Powys SY18 6EB
Tel: 01686 413916
International body that certificates sustainable timber

James Latham plc
Leeside Wharf, Mount Pleasant Hill,
London E5 9NG
Tel: 020 8806 3333
Hardwood, softwood and panel products, including MDF, flexible plywood, veneered panels

Junckers Ltd
Wheaton Court Commercial Centre,
Wheaton Road, Witham, Essex
CM8 3UJ
Tel: 01376 517512
Solid hardwood pre-finished flooring

Kahrs (UK) Ltd
Unit 2 West, 68 Bognor Road,
Chichester, West Sussex PO19 2NS
Tel: 01243 778747
Wooden flooring from sustainable sources

LASSCO Flooring
Maltby Street, Bermondsey,
London SE1 3PA
Tel: 020 7237 4488
Antique, reclaimed and new timber flooring in strip, parquet and board

Machells & Sons Ltd
Low Mills, Guiseley, Leeds,
West Yorkshire LS20 9LT
Tel: 01132 505043
Fax: 01132 500315
Recycled building materials and period features

Perstorp Surface Materials (UK) Ltd
Aycliffe Industrial Park, Newton
Aycliffe, Co Durham DL5 6EF
Tel: 08705 143022
'Pergo' laminate flooring from Sweden

Plyboo (UK) Ltd
55-57 Main Street, Alford,
Aberdeenshire AB33 8AA
Tel: 019755 63388
Bamboo flooring and panelling

Siesta Cork Tile Co.
Unit 21, Tait Road, Gloucester
Road, Croydon, Surrey. CR0 2DP
Tel: 020 8683 4055
Fax: 020 8683 4480
Cork products for floors and walls

Solid Floors
128 St John Street,
London EC1V 4JS
Tel: 020 7251 2917
Fax: 020 7253 7419
53 Pembridge Road,
London W11 3HG
Tel: 020 7221 9166
Fax: 020 7221 8193
Hardwood flooring and fitting including exotic timbers and bamboo

Victorian Wood Works
54 River Road, Creekmouth,
Barking, IG11 0DW
Tel: 020 8534 1000
Fax: 020 8534 2000
www.victorianwoodworks.co.uk
e-mail:
sales@victorian woodworks.co.uk
Reclaimed, antique and new hardwood flooring

Stone

Attica
543 Battersea Park Road,
London SW11 3BL
Tel: 020 7738 1234
Limestone, terracotta, mosaic and hand-painted tiles

Capital Marble Design
The Pall Mall Deposit, 124-128
Barlby Road, London W10 6BL
Tel: 020 8968 5340
Washbasins in limestone, marble and granite, flooring and vitrified porcelain

Delabole Slate
Pengelly, Delabole,
Cornwall PL33 9AZ
Tel: 01840 212242
Worldwide supplier of Cornish slate

Kirkstone
128 Walham Green Court, Moore
Park Road, London SW6 4DG
Tel: 020 7381 0424
Granite, travertine, limestone, slate, ceramic, glass, mosaic

Limestone Gallery Ltd
Arch 47, South Lambeth Road,
London SW8 1SS
Tel: 020 7735 8555
Limestone floors, fireplaces, basins, baths and other bespoke limestone items

Marble Flooring Specialists Ltd
Verona House, Filwood Road,
Fishponds, Bristol BS16 3RY
Tel: 0117 9656565
Fax: 0117 9656573
Marble, granite and composite stone

Marble Arch Ltd
431&432 Gordon Business Centre,
Gordon Grove, London SE5 9DU
Tel: 020 7738 7212
Marble, granite, limestone

Paris Ceramics
583 Kings Road, London SW6 2EH
Tel: 020 7371 7778
Limestone, antique stone, terra-cotta, mosaic, ceramic wall tiles

Stone Age Ltd
19 Filmer Road, London SW6 7BU
Tel: 020 7385 7954
90 types of limestone and sandstone

Stonell Ltd
521/525 Battersea Park Road,
London SW11 3BN
Tel: 020 7738 9990
A range of natural stone

Stone Productions Ltd
7-9 East Hill, London SW18 2HT
Tel: 020 8871 9257
Marble, granite, slate, limestone

WorldMarble
St James House, Northbridge
Road, Berkhamsted HP4 1EH
Tel: 01442 876500
Marble, sandstone, granite, slate, limestone; worktops, dados, tiles, skirtings, flooring, natural stone tabletops

Brick and tile

Elon Ltd
12 Silver Road, London W12 7SG
Tel: 020 8932 3000
Fax: 020 8932 3001
Cast-iron, acrylic, and ceramic sinks, taps, drain accessories, handmade tiles

Fired Earth
Twyford Mill, Oxford Road,
Adderbury, Oxon OX17 3HP
Tel: 01295 812088
Terracotta and encaustic tiles, slate, marble, limestone and quarry tiles, ceramics, wood for floors etc, bathroom accessories and paints

Ibstock Building Products Ltd
21 Dorset Square,
London NW1 6QE
Tel: 0870 903 4013
A wide range of bricks and brick paviors

The Life Enhancing Tile Company
Unit 3B, Central Trading Estate,
Bath Road, Bristol BS4 3EH
Tel: 0117 977 4600 /
0117 907 7673
Encaustic tiles

The Mosaic Workshop
Unit B, 443-449 Holloway Road,
London N7 6LJ
Tel: 020 7263 2997
Decorative mosaics in ceramic, marble and glass

The Mosaic Studio
54 Darlinghurst Grove,
Leigh-on-Sea, Essex SS9 3LG
Tel/Fax: 01702 712111
Mosaics in glass, stone, slate, ceramics, etc. Commissioned work only

Natural Tile
150 Church Road, Redfield, Bristol
BS5 9HN England
Tel: 0117 941 3707
Fax: 0117 941 3072
Contemporary tiles in glass, metal, resin, etc. Imported tiles in handmade ceramics, natural stone, tumbled marble and terracotta

Shackerley (Holdings) Group Ltd
PO Box 20 Wigan Road, Euxton, Chorley, Lancashire PR7 6JJ
Tel: 01257 273114
Fax: 01257 262386
A wide range of ceramic slabs for bathroom and kitchen worksurfaces, glass bricks

Swedecor Ltd
Manchester Street, Hull HU3 4TX
Tel: 01482 32961
Fax: 01482 212988
Ceramic tiles, swimming-pool tiles, bespoke glazing, glass-block systems

Tantrum Design Ltd
14 Fotheringhay,
Peterborough PE8 5HZ
Tel: 01832 226019
Fax: 01832 226262
Contemporary pewter tiles and contemporary furniture using wood and metal; bespoke design service available

World's End Tiles
Silverthorne Road,
London SW8 3HE
Tel: 020 7819 2100
A wide range of ceramic tiles

Glass

Avante Bathroom Products
Unit 2, Dragon Court, Springwell Road, Leeds LS12 1EY
Tel: 0113 244 5337
Glass washbasins and glass vanity tops, mirrors, bathroom accessories

Fusion Glass Designs Ltd
365 Clapham Road,
London SW9 9BT
Tel: 020 7738 5888
Architectural and decorative glass

Hourglass
Unit 14, The Tanneries,
Brockhampton Lane, Havant,
Hampshire PO9 1JB
Tel: 02392 489900
Glass, curved glass products, unusual products: balustrades, showcases

McMillan Glass Company
The Apex, Studio D, Clapham North Business Centre, Voltaire Road, London SW4 6DH
Tel: 020 7498 0100
Fax: 020 7622 0805
Specialists in stained glass and contemporary glass artists

Luxcrete Ltd
Premier House, Disraeli Road, Park Royal, London N10 7BT
Tel: 020 8965 7292
Fax: 020 8961 6337
Glass blocks and roof lights

Pilkington United Kingdom Ltd
Prescot Road, St Helens,
Cheshire WA10 3TT
Tel: 01744 692000
A huge range of decorative glass, low-E glass and other high-specification types

J Preedy and Sons
Lamb Works, North Road,
London N7 9DP
Tel: 020 7700 0377
Design and installation of glass flooring and glass panels

Swedecor Ltd
Manchester Street, Hull, HU3 4TX
Tel: 01482 329691
Glass blocks and glass-block systems

Metal

BPM – Battersea Plumbers Merchants
39 Lavender Hill, Battersea,
London SW11 5QW
Tel/Fax: 020 7738 9475
Stainless-steel and aluminium sheets

Bragman Flett
Unit 4, 193 Garth Road, Morden, Surrey SM4 4LZ
Tel: 020 8337 1934
Kitchens, floors, stairs in all metals

Forgetec Engineering
Scatterford Smithy, Newland, Coleford, Glos. GL16 8NG
Tel: 01594 835 363
Stainless-steel sheets

Gooding Aluminium Ltd
1 British Wharf, Landmann Way,
London SE14 5RS
Tel: 020 8692 2255
Aluminium sheet flooring

Natural Tile
150 Church Road, Redfield,
Bristol BS5 9HN
Tel: 0117 941 3707
Wall and floor tiles in aluminium and glass and resin, imported handmade ceramics, stone marble and terracotta

Metalworks by Decorum
Norths Estate, West Wycombe, Buckinghamshire HP14 3BE
Tel: 01494 883901
Metal tiles in nickel, polished bronze

Zinc Counters
High Street, Markington, Harrogate, North Yorkshire HG3 3NR
Tel: 01765 677808
Zinc, pewter and copper cladding for tables, counters and fascias

Concrete and plaster

Artex-Blue Hawk
Pasture Lane, Ruddington, Nottinghamshire, NG11 6AG
Tel: 0115 945 6100
Fax: 0115 945 6041
Textured finishes, plaster moulds, decorative and conventional coving

Pallam Precast
187 West End Lane, West Hampstead, London NW6 2LJ
Tel: 020 7328 6512
Fax: 020 7328 3547
Concrete, terrazzo and allied products

Paul Davies Design
Unit 5, Parkworks, 16 Park Road, Kingston-upon-Thames, KT2 6BG
Tel: 020 8541 0838
Concrete in a huge range of finishes for worksurfaces, sinks, floors, stairs, panels. Bespoke designs

G Jackson and Sons (Classical Interiors)
Unit 19, Mitcham Industrial Estate, Streatham Road, Mitcham, Surrey CR4 2AP
Tel: 020 8685 5000
Concrete and fibrous plasterwork including columns, cornices and brackets using original 18th-century moulds

Quiligotti Terrazzo Tiles Ltd
PO Box 4, Clifton Junction, Manchester M27 8LP
Tel: 0161 794 8444
Manufacturer / installer of terrazzo

Synthetics, leather and linoleum

The Amtico Company Ltd
Kingfield Road, Coventry, Warwickshire CV6 5AA
Tel: 02476 861400
Upmarket vinyl tiles

Armstrong DLW Commercial Floors
Centurion Court, Milton Park, Abingdon, Oxfordshire OX14 4RY
Tel: 01235 831296
Plain and marbled linoleum; bespoke design service

Bill Amberg Leather Design
10 Chepstow Road,
London W2 5BD
Tel: 020 7727 3560
Leather wall panelling, flooring and upholstery, bags

Bridge of Weir Leather Company
Clydesdale Works, Bridge of Weir, Renfrewshire PA11 3LF, Scotland
Tel: 01505 612132
Fax: 01505 614964
Leather for upholstery, flooring and automotive use

Dalsouple
PO Box 140, Bridgwater, Somerset, TA5 1HT
Tel: 01984 667233
Rubber flooring in wide range of colours, textures and patterns

Deralam Laminates Ltd
Units 461/4 Walton Summit, Bamber Bridge, Preston, Lancs PR5 8AR
Tel: 01772 315 888
Metal laminates and wall cladding

Dupont Corian
McD Marketing Ltd, Dupont Corian, Maylands Avenue, Hemel Hempstead, Hertfordshire HP2 7DP
Tel: 01442 346779
Corian for worktops and counters

Eternit UK Ltd
Whaddon Road, Meldreth, nr Royston, Hertfordshire SG8 5RL
Tel: 01763 260421
Decorative laminates and cladding

First Floor (Fulham) Ltd
174 Wandsworth Bridge Road, London SW6 2UQ
Tel: 020 7736 1123
Rubber, linoleum and vinyl tiles

Forbo-Nairn Ltd
PO Box 1, Kirkcaldy, Fife, Scotland KY1 2SB
Tel: 01592 643777
Marmoleum and vinyl

Formica Ltd
Coast Road, North Shields, Tyne and Wear NE29 8RE
Tel: 0191 259 3000
Decorative laminates

Harvey Maria Ltd
Trident Business Centre,
89 Bickersteth Road,
London SW17 9SH
Tel: 020 8516 7788
www.harveymaria.co.uk
Photographic designs on PVC-coated cork-based tiles

Jaymart Rubber & Plastics Ltd
Woodlands Trading Estate, Eden Vale Road, Westbury, Wiltshire BA13 3QS
Tel: 01373 864926
Wide selection of vinyl and rubber

Marley Floors
Dickley Lane, Lenham, Maidstone, Kent ME17 2QX
Tel: 01622 854000
Manufacturer of vinyl flooring

Sinclair Till
791-793 Wandsworth Road,
London SW8 3JQ
Tel: 020 7720 0031
Linoleum; custom design service

New Zealand stockists

Capital Stone Ltd
Tel: 09443 1031
Fax: 09443 1706
Marble and granite

Winstone Glass
Tel: 0800 809 010

Auckland Glass
Tel: 09415 8995

Firth Paving
Tel: 0800 800 576
Bricks and paving

Leather Care NZ Ltd
Tel: 0800 453 284
info@leathercare.co.nz

College